CITY
NEIGHBOR

OTHER BOOKS BY
CLARA INGRAM JUDSON

DONALD McKAY

SOLDIER DOCTOR

RAILWAY ENGINEER

BOAT BUILDER

CITY NEIG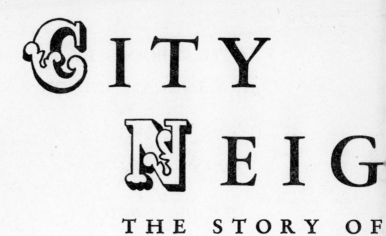

THE STORY OF

NEW YORK   1951

HBOR

JANE ADDAMS

by

CLARA INGRAM JUDSON

illustrated by

RALPH RAY

CHARLES SCRIBNER'S SONS

TO

ALICE ANNE RICE

TABLE OF CONTENTS

EPILOGUE

✄ AUTHOR'S NOTE ✄

THE MATERIAL IN THIS biography comes from three main sources: Jane Addams' own writings in letters, articles and books; newspapers, magazine articles, reports and other documents; and my own acquaintance with her.

I have used the fiction form with conversation because that seems to make her story more vivid, more as she really was. But nothing herein is fiction in the sense that an incident is imagined. Indeed, such a wealth of material is available that it is hard to choose what to omit from her story.

I am indebted to Miss Lorena M. Church of Rockford College for obtaining for me material about Jane Addams' years at Rockford and to Mr. Russell W. Ballard, Director of Hull-House, for history of the Settlement.

Clara Ingram Judson

CITY
NEIGHBOR

CHAPTER 1

✺ THE GRAY BRICK HOUSE ✺

THE LAST ECHO OF THE hall clock's mellow chime, striking midnight, faded away. There was no moon this night, and the gray brick house where John Addams and his children lived was dark and silent under the Norway pines. From the east window the barn loomed big and square in the starlight. That was where the trouble began—with the new kittens.

Six-year-old Jane stirred restlessly and pulled the covers higher under her chin.

"I *must* go to sleep!" she told herself. Thought of her father and of his firm words, "Nights are for sleeping, Jane!" made her shut her eyes tightly. But they would pop open again. She was wide awake to her toes, miserable about a moral problem too hard for a motherless little girl. In an effort to please her father, the most important person in her world, Jane had hastily told a lie. Did he know? No matter, Jane knew. And she knew, too, that he hated an untruth. What should she do?

"Why did I tell that silly lie?" she wondered miserably as the scene of the afternoon came back to her. "Father lifted me from the buggy. He told me to go straight into the house and I meant to. Then I saw Sophrina and her new kittens" . . . Memory of the baby kittens and their soft appealing ways made her smile—then she frowned quickly, overcome again by what had followed.

"I did come into the house soon—but not until I was cold. Father saw me in the kitchen," Jane thought.

"You look very cold, Jane," he had said. "Did you come directly into the house?"

"I should have said, 'I stopped a little with the kittens, Father.' But I did say: 'Yes Father. I came right in.'" Hot shame warmed her and she pushed the covers away.

The tree nearest Alice's room rubbed the eaves with a harsh sound. Jane cringed and pulled the covers back quickly. If she could only speak to her father, she thought. But the idea of going through that big silent house seemed appalling.

The house was full of people. Mary Addams, the oldest sister, slept in the room next to Jane. Martha, the pretty sister, was in the room on the other side. Martha had recently come home, very ill, from Rockford Seminary. Alice, the strong athletic sister, had a room down the hall and fourteen-year-old Weber, the only brother, had the room across from her. Polly, the nurse, was in the little room at the corner. Yes, people were there—but their doors were closed.

Polly would be quick with comfort, Jane knew, but only her father could forgive a wrong and his room was downstairs under Jane's. It seemed far away in the darkness.

"But I cannot sleep until I tell Father I am sorry," Jane thought. To get to him, she must open her door into the dark hall, go to the stairs and down—down— her heart thumped at what she must face at the stairs' end.

The hall would be dark. The front door would be unlocked—a Quaker ideal of hospitality which her father followed. Long panels of red glass at either side of the door let in a weird light. Sometimes a visitor stood by a panel and the effect was painful to Jane, even in daytime. Would someone be standing there, now, peering in?

Suddenly Jane knew that whatever lay in her way, she must see her father. She tossed covers aside and leaped out of bed. Without groping for slippers or the warm robe Polly always laid near, Jane ran to the hall door.

Perhaps if she hurried, she would not have time to be frightened.

The rough weave of the red ingrain carpet tickled her bare feet but she hardly noticed as she crept down the stairs. On the bottom step she paused, clinging to the newel post fearfully.

The oilcloth rug just below would be icy to her feet but she did not think of that. Her eyes were on the doorknob—would it turn? Was an unknown intruder standing just outside? Would she see a strange face, peering in through the red panel? Starlight made faint, moving shadows as trees near the front door swayed gently. Jane stood and stared at that knob.

It did not turn.

With one quick leap she cleared the last step, darted by the door, ran through the living room, and threw herself onto her father's bed.

"I told you a lie, Father!" she cried, clutching his shoulder. "I *didn't* come into the house directly. I stayed to play with Sophrina's kittens. When you saw that I was cold, I knew I had disobeyed—but I hoped you wouldn't know. I spoke that lie so quickly, Father, I didn't stop to think. Can you forgive me?" Words poured out eagerly now that she had come.

Her father's hand reached out and held her cold fingers.

"If my daughter tells a lie, I am glad she cannot sleep until she has set the matter right. Coming down to me may make you remember this night, Jennie, for I know

you have been afraid of the dark. But you must fear an untruth more than you fear darkness. Will you remember this, daughter?"

"I shall remember always," Jane promised solemnly. "I shall never tell a lie again. And I shall not be afraid of the dark, either—you shall see, Father."

"Now go back to bed," Mr. Addams said as he released her hands. "Good night, Jennie."

"Good night, Father."

Jane retraced her steps. She passed that front door without a glance, and climbed the stairs. Her father, the most important person in her world, had forgiven her. Never again would she speak an untruth—not even a small bit of an untruth. The day came, years later, when Jane Addams said that this midnight journey downstairs was the most important event in her childhood. When a temptation came to modify facts, even for a good reason, she thought of that night and was not tempted. And darkness never again made her afraid.

All that was far ahead, though, as a relieved and happy little girl tumbled into bed and went straight to sleep.

When she wakened, the sun was shining. Smells of frying ham drifted under her door, and sounds of activity told Jane that breakfast would soon be ready. She got out of bed and pulled the covers back over a chair to air, as Mary had taught her to do. Then she dressed quickly.

The family were gathering in the cheerful east dining room at the end of the downstairs hall.

"Good morning, Jennie," Mary said, and looked at her

closely. Since their mother's death four years before, Mary had felt responsible for this much younger sister.

The little girl coming into the dining room was small for her age. Because of an obscure spinal trouble, she held her head slightly to one side and walked pigeon-toed. (This habit worried grownups in this year 1866 for children were then taught to turn their toes *out*.) The child's widely-spaced gray eyes were serious; her brown hair was parted in the middle in the fashion of the day. Jane was inclined to be self-conscious, and she thought the concern that Mary and the others had about her showed that she was ugly and troublesome to them. Now she flushed and hurried to her place at the table as Polly came from the kitchen.

"You're to eat all of this oatmeal, Jennie," Polly announced as she set a bowlful in front of Jane. "I put rich cream and maple sugar on it. You are to show me the bottom of the bowl before you get your ham and eggs."

"All that, Polly!" Jane exclaimed. "But it does smell good. I'm hungry."

"Good reason!" Polly grunted. "You ate no supper last night."

"Good morning, Weber," Polly went on. "I won't have to coax you to eat! Sit down and I'll bring your breakfast, too."

In the stir of breakfast and getting Alice and Weber off to school in Freeport, six miles away, Jane finished her breakfast unnoticed.

The Addams home and the two mills were close to

Cedarville, a small village in northwestern Illinois. By next year, Jane would probably start her education at the village school there, as the others had. For the upper grades they had to drive into Freeport. At the present, Jane spent her days around the house and the mills or in the big barn. Of course she helped her sisters and did her knitting. The house was a big one for that time and place. Mr. Addams had built it soon after he and his bride had moved west from Pennsylvania.

John Addams had prospered in Illinois. His good judgment, his thrift and industry had rewarded him. His farm, his sawmill and gristmill made him a good living and he was respected in the community. There was no Quaker church near, so the children went to the village Sunday school and to the nearby churches in turn. Mr. Addams had confidence in his way of living and he was strict with his children, determined to bring them up well.

Jane's health often worried him, especially now that Martha was ill, too. He thought Jane needed more fresh air, so he often took her with him when he did business errands with neighboring farmers or in town. Jane liked these drives. Driving was much more fun than playing alone.

A couple of mornings after Jane's midnight dash to her father, he came through the kitchen while she was polishing spoons at the big table.

"Want to drive to town with me, Jennie?" he asked.

"Oh, Father, I *do*!" she answered happily. "I'll get my

bonnet quickly."

"No hurry. I have to hitch up," he told her. "Better give her a glass of milk, Polly. She's such a thin little sparrow." And he went on to the barn.

Polly turned to get the milk.

"I'll spread a piece of bread and butter and brown sugar, Jennie. You like that." She did not notice the sudden look of sadness that came into the little girl's face.

"They think I am an ugly little girl," she thought. "Father is ashamed of me." She wished that she could stay at home.

But she ate and drank and ran to the barn where her father was hitching the horses and when they were on their way she forgot about herself. And soon they were in Freeport.

"This is not the street we usually take, Father," Jane observed.

"No, and it doesn't go by the candy store, either," her father teased. "My first errand is in this mill end of town. I want to see why Fred didn't come back to work. Later we shall go to Main Street."

As they drove along Jane looked around with increasing distaste.

"I don't like these horrid little houses, Father!" she exclaimed. "I never knew Freeport had houses like these. Look at that one! The front steps are broken. The paint is peeling off. The yard is cluttered with trash. Our yard isn't like that. Why do people live in such ugly places?"

"Oh for many reasons," her father answered. "Probably there is not enough money for a better place. Likely the family rent and do not bother to keep it tidy. Landlords are careless, too. No one seems to care. Possibly some of these people have never lived in a better place and so do not mind as you do.

"And people are poor. Poverty is never pretty, Jane. Here we are. Now you sit quietly while I talk to Fred."

He stopped the horses, wound the reins around the whip socket and climbed out. Then he fastened a weighted strap to the nearest horse's bit. There was no hitch-post or carriage block here, as at the Addams home. The weight by the front wheel would remind the horses to stand quietly.

While he was in the house, Jane watched a group of children playing in the untidy yard. They seemed to be enjoying themselves. But the yard was so dirty that she felt uncomfortable for them. She was glad when her father returned.

"They have a horrid yard, Father," she told him as they drove away. "I think children should have a nice place to play."

Her father said nothing. His mind was on his business.

"When I am grown," Jane spoke with vigor that caught his attention, "I shall live in a nice, big house, like ours. But I shall have my house near little houses. Then I shall invite all the children to come and play in my yard."

Mr. Addams looked down at her anxiously. Jane certainly was a serious child. She needed playmates, but no families with children lived near the Addams home. He hardly knew what to do about her.

"When you are grown you may find many other things to do, daughter," he remarked. He shook the reins in annoyance and drove briskly to Main Street.

While her father did his errands at the bank and stores, Jane sat in the buggy, thinking about those mill children. Their tiny house would have no big cheerful kitchen, with a Polly bustling about cooking savory meals. They had no pine shaded yard sloping to a dashing little creek. There was no big barn with kittens, horses and cows. Why didn't all children have these things, the same as she had? She had never thought about this before and now that she did, the idea worried her. Something was wrong, she felt.

"Poverty is never pretty," her father had said. Jane could not remember ever hearing that word before. If 'poverty' meant a grubby yard and tumbled-down house, well, she did not like poverty.

Mr. Addams came from the store and they started for home. Nothing more was said about children or houses. Her father enjoyed driving and he let the horses out. They fairly flew over the road to reach home in time for dinner.

But though nothing more was said, Jane did not forget that house and yard. Nights when her back hurt she thought about it. Why didn't people *do* something? That was the puzzle. Then from day to day other things happened and the picture was pushed back in her mind. But it was never really forgotten.

CHAPTER 2

∽ JANE'S NEW FAMILY ∾

IN HER EIGHTH YEAR something happened which changed Jane's life. Her father married the widow of his good friend, William Haldeman, and the new Mrs. Addams brought her two sons with her to live in the gray brick house. The older boy, Harry Haldeman, was eighteen and, like Jane's own brother and sisters, he was busy with his education. George Haldeman was six months younger than Jane and he proved to be a fine companion for the shy, lonely girl.

The new mother was not fearful for Jane as Mary and Alice and Polly were. Their concern was natural enough, for beautiful Martha had died the year before, and the family lavished care upon frail little Jane. Mrs. Addams allowed Jane to run and play with George as she pleased. Sometimes Jane's back did hurt terribly, but on the whole her health and spirits improved. She learned to laugh and she gradually stopped pondering deep thoughts in the night. And she no longer worried about her appearance, for George frankly liked her as she was.

Mrs. Addams had a hobby of reading plays and she was a good musician, playing the guitar and the piano. Jane was never musical but she learned to enjoy good music. And perhaps best of all, Mrs. Addams liked diversion and was always ready for a trip or a party—Jane had never known such good times.

On a June day, Jane and George spent the morning collecting butterflies in the meadow beyond the barn. Suddenly, Jane stood quietly and studied the sky.

"What are you looking for, Jennie?" George asked. He, too, stopped running and looked up. But he could see nothing interesting—just a few specks off to the north.

"Likely those are eagles," he said casually and swung his butterfly net again. Eagles were common in Illinois at that time.

"One of those might be Old Abe, Jane said hopefully and she watched the specks get smaller and smaller in the distance.

"Old Abe sounds like Abraham Lincoln and he is dead," George told her in a superior tone.

"I know he is," Jane retorted impatiently. "I am older than you are. I remember the day he died. The Old Abe I am looking for is an eagle. He is named for the president because people called Mr. Lincoln 'Old Abe' before he was elected. My father told me, and he knew Mr. Lincoln."

"What is this Old Abe eagle?" George asked, not much interested, being hot and hungry.

"He was a mascot for a regiment from Wisconsin," Jane explained. "My teacher said that sometimes he flies away from his home and then, after a while, flies back because he is used to being cared for. She said maybe we could see him, if we watch. I would like to see him."

"I would rather eat dinner than see any old eagle," George decided.

"We can ask Father if it is true that the eagle flies away," Jane agreed. She was hungry, too, so they trudged on home.

At dinner, Mr. Addams was doubtful about the eagle flying free.

"Old Abe belongs to the Eighth Wisconsin Regiment," he said. "The men carried him through the war and brought him safely back to Madison. He was their good luck—their mascot. I never heard that he flies off, as you say."

"But the war ended three years ago!" George exclaimed. "The eagle can't still be alive?"

Mr. Addams smiled at George's idea of a long time.

"He is very much alive and cared for by two soldiers. I am told that hundreds of people come to see him."

"Oh, I wish I could see Old Abe, Father!" Jane said it as one would say, 'I'd like to visit the moon,' expecting nothing.

"You have a good idea, Jennie," Mrs. Addams spoke briskly, "Madison is only sixty-five miles away. A trip there would make a nice outing to celebrate Alice's homecoming. Let's go and take the children, John." She turned and spoke to her husband so casually that Jane was astonished. The most amazing things had happened since the new mother had come—and now a journey.

"Will that eagle look like the picture in the parlor?" George asked as he passed his plate for more pudding. "Please give me lots of sauce, Mother. I like lemon sauce."

"Perhaps not exactly the same," Mr. Addams answered. He had learned that George was observing of birds. "The picture represents an American eagle, but not this particular bird. The men in that picture were a Cedarville Company and the eagle was put above them as a symbol of a strong union."

"Father outfitted that company," Jane told George proudly. "That's why they were called the Addams Guards."

After dinner they went into the parlor. Mr. Addams lifted Jane and then George so they could study the pictured eagle hung high on the wall above other war pictures.

"I shall like to see a real eagle," George decided. The children talked of that trip continually and made plans.

On a beautiful midsummer day a fortnight later, the party of five, Mr. and Mrs. Addams, Alice, now home from Rockford Seminary, and Jane and George set out in the family carriage for Madison. Fields had the golden sheen of freshly cut wheat stubble and the gathered grain lay in great yellow piles awaiting the threshers. Woods were still a deep green and roadside bushes were laden with luscious wild berries.

The journey was to take two days each way. They would stop over night with friends, midway, and stay a night in a hotel in Madison. The children were agog with excitement, and to keep them quiet Mr. Addams told them tales about his friend Abraham Lincoln. John Addams had been a state senator since 1854 and during the fifties, before Lincoln went to Washington, he knew the man well and they often corresponded.

"I have some letters from Mr. Lincoln which I must show you when we get home," Mr. Addams said as they drove up and down the hills. "Mr. Lincoln usually began a letter to me 'Dear Double-D-ed Addams.' He liked to tease me about that extra letter our ancestor put in the name."

"*Why* did he do that?" George interrupted.

Jane glanced at her stepbrother uneasily. Her father hated interruptions. Now he would be annoyed and this nice outing might be spoiled. But Mr. Addams had his mind on his driving and his tale and appeared not to notice for he replied to George without even a reproof.

"Oh, there were two young second cousins in the neighborhood there in Pennsylvania and both were named Isaac Adams. One put an extra d in his name to stop the confusion and his descendents kept it.

"One thing I always liked about Mr. Lincoln—he never wrote to ask for favors as many men did. His letters were about state business or to ask my opinion about some party matter."

"You cried the day Mr. Lincoln died," Jane said, when

her father paused.

"Did I, Jennie?" Mr. Addams was surprised that she had noticed. "The death of a great man is a sad event—and Mr. Lincoln was so needed to lead the nation out of the misery of war."

"And I remember that our front gate was decorated with two flags," Jane added. "You tied them with black bands of crepe."

"Imagine a child not yet five remembering that!" Mrs. Addams said briskly. "I see a nice place for eating our lunch, ahead on the hilltop, John.

"George, you help with the feed bags while Alice and Jane and I unpack the basket."

Mr. Addams pulled the carriage off the road, and they climbed out stiffly. Mrs. Addams unfolded a red-and-white checked tablecloth and spread it on the grass. Mr. Addams laid carriage robes beside it and then put feed bags on the horses so they could munch at leisure. Soon the travelers were enjoying fried chicken, hard boiled eggs, sugared rusks, homemade pickles, pound cake, and early plums from the home orchard.

The arrival in Madison the next afternoon was thrilling. The Capitol was the largest building the children had ever seen. It sparkled whitely in the afternoon sunshine and its dome seemed to touch the sky. The next morning they visited Old Abe and found him as old and big and shaggy as they had expected. The keeper on duty was dressed in a shabby army coat. He allowed the two children to stand close to the bar where the eagle perched

and the great bird preened himself and blinked at them knowingly.

"That old fellow was in thirty-six battles or skirmishes," the keeper boasted. "Men fell dead all around him and he never got a scratch. He's a lucky one, that bird." He touched the feathers gently and the bird snapped at him good-naturedly. The children were entranced.

Probably Mr. Lincoln never saw that eagle—the old soldier would have boasted of it if he had. But somehow the sight of that great bird, a symbol of strength, seemed to make tales of the martyred president more real than before. The children were thoughtful as they followed Mr. Addams from the building.

At the top of the white marble steps he paused to speak to them.

"You must never forget," he said, "that Mr. Lincoln believed in the American form of government. He thought that it could make a better world. He believed that every man should be equal under the law. Mr. Lincoln held that ideal before the nation, as the soldiers held the great eagle before the regiment. We must make this ideal come true."

Jane and George listened solemnly. They would never forget that scene on the wide steps. After they returned home, they had a new respect for pictures of the Lincoln-Douglas debate which had been held in Freeport and for other Lincoln pictures that hung in the parlor.

In the autumn Jane and George went together to the village school, where Mr. Samuel Parr did his best for them. Jane studied Latin and English along with the usual arithmetic, reading, and spelling. George liked nature study better than Latin, though he took both, and he told Jane that when he was grown he meant to study nature and discover facts that no one else knew.

George Haldeman was a practical boy who liked to see and handle objects. He collected bugs and butterflies, birds' eggs and snakes, worms, and cocoons. He was willing to roam the hills for hours in search of treasure. Jane usually went with him and soon was making collections of her own.

On rainy days they played in the mills. At first, the flour mill was their favorite place, and they made up games to play in empty bins. But as they grew older they played in the sawmill where there was the excitement of real danger. George would leap astride a log as it approached the whirling saw—Jane watching in fascination and horror. Then, barely in the nick of time, he would spring off. The whine of the saw as it struck the log covered the children's shrieks of glee, and the grownups never discovered this sport.

As Jane grew older, she was encouraged to supplement her school work by reading at home. When she got through the *Iliad, Virgil* and a *History of the World* the joy of reading began to pall, so Mr. Addams offered her five cents, each, for reading *Plutarch's Lives*. Jane began, only to find that mere reading the volume was not enough. She must stand before her father, give him a review of the book and answer any questions he chose to ask. She got that first nickel and finished the "Lives." After that she searched the shelves for a book that he had not read—but in vain! He seemed to know the contents of every book!

By the time Jane was sixteen, she had made up her mind that she wanted to go to college and get a degree. This was unusual for a girl of that time and place, and Mr. Addams was none too pleased. He had recently been elected a trustee of Rockford Female Seminary, at Rockford, Illinois. Alice had graduated from Rockford in 1872, four years before, and Mary had attended the Seminary during Alice's senior year. Mr. Addams was well pleased with the Seminary and expected Jane to go there and then complete her education with travel.

Jane, however, was determined to have a degree, and she proposed to get it at Smith College in Northampton, Massachusetts. That seemed a long way from home to Mr. Addams. He let the matter drift, thinking that it was merely a girl's dream.

Mrs. Addams was ambitious and liked the idea of Jane going East. Alice and her stepbrother Harry had recently married—now Mrs. Addams had match-making notions about George and Jane. How nice it would be to have George's wife acquire an eastern degree! She encouraged Jane to dream.

May came, and Jane was studying long hours for the entrance examinations. These were oral and given only at Northampton. Jane worried as she studied, for her father had not given his consent. Mrs. Addams came to her aid and talked privately with her husband.

"Why don't you let Jane go?" she suggested. "The trip will be diverting for her, John, and educational, too."

"Um-m—if she failed to pass she would see how silly the whole idea is," he said.

So Jane went East and took the terrifying examinations. In July, word came to Cedarville that she had passed and was accepted for entrance at Smith College.

Mr. Addams was astounded—pride in her scholarship mingled with dismay.

"If I send a daughter East I must resign my trusteeship," he said to his wife. "I should feel a cheat if I failed to support the Seminary when I am on its board." To

Jane, he made no such explanation—fathers did not explain in those days.

"I have thought it over, Jane," he merely announced, "and you are to go to Rockford in the fall."

Jane loved him too much to object. She knew that she could get a fine education at Rockford and she had learned that in its charter the Seminary had the right to award a full college degree. That was a cause to work for!

CHAPTER 3

∽ COLLEGE DAYS ∾

A FEW DAYS LATER, MR. Addams handed his daughter a catalogue from Rockford Seminary. She opened it at once and began reading.

"It sounds as though I shall have to take entrance examinations all over again!" Jane exclaimed.

"Naturally," Mr. Addams replied. "You could not expect us to accept the verdict of others. You will take them when you arrive in the fall."

"These are written—I shall have to be examined in— in eight subjects!" Jane could hardly believe the words she read. "I must start reviewing immediately."

"Does the catalogue tell what you are to bring with you?" Mrs. Addams asked.

Jane turned a page. "Tuition is $175 a year. Extras are $6 for gas light; $5 for rent of the carpet in the student's room. Fuel at cost—"

"No need to spend money for wood," Mr. Addams interrupted. "I can bring it in the buggy when I come to the trustees' meetings. And I shall see to it that you buy the furniture left in the room by the former student."

Jane continued reading. "Each student is to bring a knife, fork and teaspoon; napkins, bed linen and blankets; towels and a year's supply of plain, inexpensive clothing, especially flannels. One pair of India Rubber overshoes, a waterproof cloak and an umbrella are required." She looked up in surprise.

"Miss Sill insists that the students walk an hour each day, rain or shine," Mr. Addams explained. "She finds that such exercise improves the health."

"Students are requested to bring no jewelry," Jane read on, "and all articles must be marked with the owner's full name. Weekly accounting of expenditures is required and each student must bring a letter of introduction from her parents."

"Miss Sill knows you are coming," Mr. Addams said with some pride, "but we shall follow all rules."

Her father's pride was a challenge to Jane. She must, she simply must, pass those entrance examinations with credit to him. She set herself a rigid program of study which was interrupted only when George begged for her company on a canter through the woods and over the hills on their favorite horses. George was going to Beloit College in the fall; he was a fair student but had no driving urge, such as possessed Jane.

Rockford Female Seminary was already thirty years old that autumn of 1877 when Jane Addams lifted her bags and bundles from the buggy and entered the door of

Middle Hall. She passed her examinations with credit and was assigned to a second floor room on the west side of one of three red brick buildings. From the windows she could see Rock River and many of the factories and businesses that were already making the place more of a manufacturing center than a college town.

Her room had a bright-colored ingrain carpet, a bed, a table-desk, two chairs and a sheet-iron stove set on a zinc base for fire protection. Fire wood was piled in a woodbox nearby.

From the first day, Jane liked Rockford Seminary. Miss Sill, the principal, was austere in appearance, but Jane saw her fine character. Miss Sill presided over the two hundred girls entrusted to her with keen attention to their religion, their health, and their education.

The required hour of daily walking was fun, at first, while autumn crisped the leaves and tempted groups to walk along the river. But when winter arrived with mud and then snow, exercise was a chore. Miss Sill allowed walking on the board walk around the buildings—thirty times around each day, rain or shine. But Jane found that with good company, even that stint was not too bad. Her health improved and walking hurt her back less than horseback riding with George. She thrived on the strict regime.

About a third of the students lived in Rockford and returned to their homes after study periods. The other two thirds were of many ages because the seminary not only had the three years of advanced work, but several years of preparatory. There were also some advanced students in art and music. Among her classmates Jane soon formed a close friendship with Ellen Gates Starr, who came from the little town of Durand nearby. Whenever possible she and Ellen walked together, and studied together, and dreamed of doing great things for the world.

Miss Sill was deeply religious, and in the way of that time, she had a daily concern about students' souls. She hoped to send many of her girls out to be missionaries in the foreign missionary field.

Jane and Ellen had long talks about religion.

"Isn't it selfish to think all the time about my own soul —'saving' my soul! That's all we hear about!"

"But Jane—!" Ellen was a little shocked.

"I read my Bible every day as you do," Jane went on. "I find that Jesus said there are *two* commandments. He says we should love God—and I do. But he says, too, 'Love thy neighbor as thyself.' Perhaps my neighbor is as important as my own soul—yet I hear little about that second commandment."

"How can you say that!" Ellen exclaimed. "Miss Sill talked only this morning about our duty to convert the heathen."

"Yes, I heard," Jane admitted. "I think it *is* our duty, Ellen. I don't disagree with Miss Sill. But something in me makes me hold back—are there no people in our own state, perhaps even in this town, who need us?" They argued about it for hours all through that school year.

Next fall Ellen did not return to Rockford. She began teaching and the two friends saw each other only occasionally. But they wrote long letters and kept up a close friendship. Fortunately, Jane made a new friend in Catherine Waugh, 'Kittie' Waugh everyone called her, who entered as a freshman. Kittie was a kindred soul for Jane. She, too, was determined to have a real college degree and the two girls appointed themselves as a committee to see that they got what they wanted most.

Rockford was a prairie town, but it offered many advantages to students aside from fine teachers and good courses. Visiting lecturers came from the East—Bronson Alcott was one of the more popular of these—and at such times the Seminary entertained lavishly. The menu for one of these banquets included such tasty delicacies as "Escalloped oysters, Lobster à la Amerique, Buffalo Tongue, Bisquit Glace."

From Monday morning until Friday afternoon, days were crowded with work. Studies, care of their rooms, walks, filled every hour. But on Friday evenings and Saturdays, the students had many diversions. Jane's sister Mary had married John Linn, a Presbyterian minister. His church was in a village about eight miles from the Seminary and often John drove over to fetch Jane for a brief visit. On other Saturdays, George came down from Beloit College and brought a friend with him. Beloit was near so they could drive in George's buggy or in a sleigh and so provide the treat of a ride for Jane and a friend.

One of the boys who came with George was Rollin

Salesbury, who promptly fell head over heels in love with Jane and wanted to be engaged immediately. This did not endear him to George who wanted to be engaged to Jane himself. But since Jane would not be engaged to either young man and said so quite firmly, the two continued to be friends—and to visit at the Seminary whenever they were allowed.

Other week ends Jane invited a friend to go with her to Cedarville. Mrs. Addams usually planned so that George and Rollin came home at the same time, and the household was gay. Weber, who had chosen Ann Arbor for his education, was now married and living on a farm nearby. Alice and Harry Haldeman had moved to Iowa and Mr. and Mrs. Addams welcomed company. Mrs. Addams looked after the girls' clothes and manners and entertained them with delicious meals and good music. But, of course, such trips away were relatively few.

Sunday morning at college was Jane's favorite time of the whole week. It was "clearing up time" when drawers and desks were tidied ready for inspection. This was not the weekly cleaning with broom and window washing; that was a Saturday task. This was quieter work, when one made plans for the coming week, and put desk and papers in order.

Jane always got up early and hurried with her tasks so that she could have an hour before church with her favorite teacher, Miss Blaisdell. Together they read in Miss Blaisdell's Greek Testament and together they tried to understand the full religious meaning of the original

Greek. One morning there was a surprise for Jane, a Greek New Testament inscribed to Jane Addams, a gift from Miss Blaisdell's brother, who was on the faculty at Beloit.

Two literary societies at the Seminary contested hotly for members. Jane joined the Casperians, who scorned working for "marks" and asserted that they acquired knowledge for its own sake. The Vesperians, too, had lofty ideals and both societies acquired desirable members. The campaign ended with a play which Jane wrote.

Jane enjoyed writing. In her freshman year a few of her articles were published in the student paper, the *Rockford Seminary Magazine.* During the next two years she was the editor of its "Home Department." This section of the paper, a quarterly, was supposed to have jokes and anecdotes, but like most writing of that time, was ponderous and elegant. In Jane's senior year the paper had become a monthly and she the editor-in-chief. For the first time in its history the magazine paid its own way.

There was a science club, too. Jane grew wheat in a pan under her stove, and her window sills were cluttered with glasses filled with sprouting seeds. Visiting lecturers talked of the wonders of science, and the girls petitioned for more courses.

George was keenly interested in Jane's experiments in botany. He planned to prepare himself to be a research biologist and soon Jane found herself announcing that she meant to be a doctor and practice among the poor. Kittie Waugh had long intended to be a lawyer. At Rockford one simply had to "be" something or face disgrace as an idler.

And then came the spring of Jane's third year at the Seminary. She could graduate—with the usual certificate. But she did not value a certificate. Backed by Kittie Waugh, she told Miss Sill that she wanted further work and a full college degree.

"You have the right by charter to award it," Jane said politely, but firmly. "I want to study advanced courses— calculus, more Greek and Literature."

Miss Sill had little interest in degrees, but the girls were correct, so she agreed. Jane came back for her fourth year. She took public speaking as well as the advanced courses, and found that she enjoyed it even more than science. Kittie liked speaking, too, and between them the two girls got up several contests in declamation that year.

In the spring they decided that Rockford should be represented at the State Intercollegiate Oratorical Contest to be held that year at Jacksonville. The director of the contest wrote back in some dismay—girls had never before entered a state contest. He seemed to think that should dispose of the business. He didn't know Jane and Kittie. They were merely spurred to further effort. And grudging consent was given at the last minute—a candidate and alternate would be allowed to come to Jacksonville, at which time the final decision as to their entering would be made.

By this time the whole Seminary was excited and the hall was packed when applicants tried out for the honor of representing the Seminary. Jane, now a Senior, won, with Kittie, a Junior, as alternate. The two girls set themselves to polishing their orations and improving their delivery. Committees of students, as well as various teachers, listened to rehearsals and commented with brutal frankness. Even at the last rehearsal there were more criticisms.

"Jane drops her voice at the end of each sentence," a student objected. "She will never win. She has too many mannerisms."

"She sounds half the time as though she apologized for living!" another cried.

"I think her whole speech is too moral—too woman-ish," another said. "Men students will talk of large issues. They will flourish statistics. Why can't you, too, Jane?"

Jane, a lump in her throat, promised to rewrite certain parts of the oration and to get rid of her mannerisms. She spent most of the night rewriting and the next morning she and Kittie left for Jacksonville.

The committee, still somewhat uneasy, allowed Jane to enter, and their very reluctance so impressed Jane that she felt the whole future of women in the world of affairs rested on her tired shoulders. Moreover, Rollin Salesbury was a contestant along with a William Jennings Bryan. Nine, altogether, were entered.

When the candidates had gone, the students at Rock-ford suddenly felt assured of victory. How could Jane fail to win—had they not trained her themselves? By way of spending their feverish energy, they gathered spring flowers and wove yards of garlands to decorate the hall for the returning heroine.

"But girls," Margaret announced as the garlands piled high, "Jane cannot possibly get back until day after to-morrow—these will be dead before then!"

"Not the way I shall care for them," a Junior announced. "We'll collect all the washtubs and fill them with water. The basement is cool . . ."

"Cold, I call it," Margaret interrupted tartly.

"Yes," agreed the student, "and the flowers will keep perfectly."

But they reckoned without Jane. She did her best at the contest and came out fifth. Rollin Salesbury won and William Jennings Bryan (later called the silver-tongued orator) was second. Jane was sorry, but the others really were good, and for the first time in weeks, she felt free.

"We should not leave this town until we have seen the state institution for the blind and the deaf," she said to Kittie. So, secure in the nobility of their purpose (and knowing nothing of the garlands), they went visiting.

When they finally arrived at the Seminary the garlands were wilted and brown and enthusiasm for the returning heroine was even damper than the softened stems. Jane felt she had brought disgrace upon her school.

Fortunately commencement was just ahead—that soon turned attention from her failure.

CHAPTER 4

∾ AFTER GRADUATION ∾

O N A SUNNY JUNE DAY, that year of 1881, wagons from the country, buggies from nearer by, and hacks with visitors who came by train converged on the Seminary campus as a crowd gathered to attend the annual commencement. The three brick buildings were astir with excitement. Under classmen dashed hither and yon on vitally important missions. Graduates primped, knowing that every lock of hair, every ruffle must be in place.

The auditorium in East Hall was packed with proud parents and with students when, prompt to the minute, as Miss Sill always was, the faculty and graduates marched on the platform to music played on the little piano Miss Sill had brought West by wagon, years before. The Rockford newspaper gave columns of space, next day, to the exercises and to Jane Addams's address. She had earned the proud honor of Valedictorian by her high grades—an honor that dispelled the failure at Jackson-

34

ville. The newspaper story was headed:

"Seventeen Buds of Blooming Promise
make their bow to Alma Mater
and their debut before the world."

There was music and the reading of graduation essays; then Jane rose to make the farewell address to the town and the faculty. To the citizens of Rockford she said:

"In a quiet part of your busy city for four years a class of girls has lived, studied some, planned and dreamed much more." She thanked them for kindnesses.

She spoke warmly of Miss Sill, "our honored principal," and said that the class appreciated her personality and the high social service she was rendering.

Miss Blaisdell was retiring, and Jane thanked her for her skilful teaching and said, "With the hard lessons of Latin and Greek you have taught us the harder lessons of thoroughness and uprightness."

Jane ended her talk gracefully—"I will only say 'God be with you' which is the older and better form of 'Good-bye.' "

The graduates received their certificates and Miss Sill announced that one, Jane Addams, had qualified for a college degree and in due time, perhaps at next year's commencement, it would be awarded.

Four happy years were ended. In a flurry of farewells and ardent promises not to forget their ideals and pledges to do something for the world, the class of 1881 left for home.

When Jane unpacked back in her room in Cedarville, she came across a copy of the *Seminary Magazine* and an article she had written that spring. Now, as she sat at the window overlooking the big barn she reread her own words.

"Always do what you are afraid to do! Once I believed that. Now I know that to do what you are afraid to do is to have your life guided by fear. How much better not to be afraid to do what you believe in doing! Keep one main idea, and you will never be lost."

But how was she to keep to an idea—here, in quiet Cedarville? And what was her objective? Kittie Waugh was fortunate. She knew without any doubt that on graduation she would study law. Jane had no such driving ambition to study medicine. But the thought of caring for those who were sick and poor appealed. She wrote to the Woman's Medical College at Philadelphia enclosing records she had brought from the Seminary and she was accepted to enter as a freshman in the fall.

July passed quickly and pleasantly. George was at home and full of plans for his studies at Johns Hopkins University in Baltimore, Maryland. Mrs. Addams filled the house with young people and gay parties.

In August, Mr. Addams took his wife and Jane and George to northern Michigan. He was considering the purchase of some property in the mining region, and a tour of inspection would give them all a good vacation. In the midst of the happy journey he was suddenly taken ill. They got him to Green Bay, Wisconsin, where he died, quite suddenly, a few hours later. In those days nothing could be done to check acute appendicitis.

Jane kept up and returned home with the others. She saw her father buried in the little cemetery across the creek by the side of her mother and Martha and the three babies who had died before Jane was born. But as she walked back, across the creek and up the hill her world suddenly collapsed.

She had tried so hard, all her life, to be what her dominating father wished her to be. Now when he was suddenly gone, her life seemed to fall to pieces like a house without a foundation. She did not know what she, herself, was, or thought, or wished to become . . . For days she hardly knew what was done or said around her.

Goldenrod in the meadow turned brown and stiff. Here and there leaves were drifting into fence corners. But Jane had not noticed the flight of time, until the day she came into the dining room and heard George and his mother talking about railway tickets. It was September and George was leaving Monday for Johns Hopkins!

"But I was going East, too!" Jane exclaimed. "You can't leave me here, George!"

George brightened, but his mother was cautious.

"You look so white and ill, Jane," she said. "How can you study—off in a strange place?"

"I shall be better," Jane exclaimed. "I shall stop sitting around feeling sorry for myself. I shall go when George does—you'll help me, won't you?"

She convinced them, so a seamstress was fetched from Freeport and Jane's clothes were put in order and packed. Jane tried to laugh and joke. Food was of little interest but somehow she got it down. Fortunately arrangements had been made; she only had to write, telling the time of her arrival. And so the two left Cedarville, happy as brother and sister and friends, but not engaged as Mrs. Addams and George had so hoped they would be. Jane thought it fortunate that this living in the same house was to end.

Jane plunged into her new work, glad to be rid of the emptiness of the Cedarville house. George came over every week or two. He was engrossed in his work and very happy. Jane slowly came to realize that she had no such joy in her courses in anatomy as George had in biology. She studied hard, thinking that with application her interest would grow,—but it did not. She was given high marks for her seven months course and was about to go on when suddenly she was very ill.

Her spine, never quite right, now gave serious trouble and for weeks Jane lay ill in that Philadelphia hospital. Her journey home, later, was a nightmare of misery.

A letter from Kittie Waugh arrived the next day.

"Only a fortnight, now," Kittie wrote, "and we shall both have our degrees! Isn't it WONDERFUL!" Jane sighed. Once that degree had seemed important. Now, she was thankful if she could sit up an hour without misery.

But the letter had been a good thing. It inspired Jane

with determination to get to Kittie's commencement. Until the last day such a risk seemed impossible—but she went. Moreover, she stood up straight and accepted that roll of parchment that said Jane Addams was now a Bachelor of Arts. The girls flocked around her, proud to know a graduate who had finished a year in medical school. Jane accepted their friendliness; she did not tell them what she now knew—that she could not go back to medical college. She did not say that perhaps she could never do any of the noble things they had dreamed.

She got home—and then was ill again for weeks. Nerve and ambition could hold her up for a time, but they were no cure.

Harry Haldeman, now Dr. Haldeman, of Mitchelville, Iowa, had been writing to his mother about Jane and her illness. Now Alice wrote to Jane.

"Harry thinks you should come out here, Jane. He has an idea that he can help you and he is being very successful. Do manage someway to come and let him try to cure you. I shall be glad to nurse you, Sister. Anyway, we shall have a good visit."

The kindly, hopeful words comforted Jane. The trip was tedious and painful but she arrived safely and after she had rested, Harry studied her back.

"I think you have an abscess on your spine, Jane," he said slowly. "I think I can remove it. But recovery may be slow—I wonder—"

"If you think you can help me—what are we waiting for?" Jane asked briskly.

The operation was successful and Harry was right, too, about the slow convalescence. Jane had to lie on a board for six months and then wear a heavy brace made of steel and whalebone for more than a year.

She was wearing the brace when Dr. Harry came into his house one noon carrying an open letter.

"I didn't tell you until I heard what Mother thought of the idea," he began.

"Now Harry!" Alice exclaimed, "You're up to something!"

Harry winked at Jane. "She thinks she knows me!" He laughed. "You are going to Europe, Jane, you and Mother. And you are to stay until you are well and strong."

Jane stared at him, speechless with astonishment.

"A sea voyage!" Alice cried, "Why didn't I think of that myself? *May* she, Harry?"

"Yes, if she is not too strenuous." Harry was watching Jane's flushed, happy face. "Mother knows you must travel slowly. You will visit relatives in Pennsylvania, and perhaps some cousins and their friends will go with you so you will have young companionship."

The plan turned out as Harry had predicted. In August six girls, with Mrs. Addams as chaperon, sailed on the *Servia*. Like a true tourist Jane kept a diary and recorded that Theodore Thomas, Henry James and other celebrities were on their ship. They stopped in Ireland and visited Blarney Castle. They "did" Scotland and the Lake region in England and then arrived in London where they took lodgings and leisurely began to enjoy the city.

On a Saturday evening, not long after their arrival in London, they chanced to go on a sightseeing tour that changed Jane's life. She wrote a little about it in her note book under that date.

"We took the underground to Aldersgate Street, then an omnibus (on top) to Bethnal Green. We came back by the Mile End Road to the station near the old debtors' prison. Thousands of poor people who were marketing at stalls along the streets . . . gave me the impression of the wretchedness of East London. And I saw for the first time the overcrowded quarters of a great city at midnight."

This section of London, the East End, had the doubtful honor of being considered the worst slum area in the world. Visitors, like the Addams party, were taken to gaze at the sights. Jane was so moved that she could not write more in her diary, but later she recounted the story of what they saw.

The bus had paused and swung half way around so passengers could look down the street where crowds surrounded two carts.

"We have a city ordinance," the driver explained, "that forbids the sale of food on the Sabbath. Of course fruit and vegetables will not keep over Sunday so hucksters buy them and auction them off. Quite a sight—look!"

A sight indeed! Jane Addams had never seen such *people,* such *clothing*! Old men, haggard and unshaven; old women with dirty, gray hair streaming over gaunt cheeks; mothers holding babies—mothers who probably were young but who looked old, worn with hunger and misery. Their clothing was incredible—ragged, ill-fitting, filthy.

" 'Ow much?" the auctioneer yelled and waved a bunch of wilted greens.

A hundred hands—old hands, bony hands, lean young hands, reached out to clutch the greens. Scores of hoarse voices made a blur of sound, Jane could hardly distinguish words. The auctioneer scornfully tossed the greens to his left and pocketed the coin handed to him.

" 'Ow much?" The scene was enacted again, this time with a half-rotten cabbage.

" 'Arf penny!" "Farthing!" Now Jane could catch a few of the shouted bids.

"Done!" The auctioneer tossed the cabbage to a man on the edge of the crowd. The buyer lunged—and missed. The cabbage fell into the gutter and a look of anguish came to the man's face—would his prize be trampled underfoot? He pushed forward and rescued the cabbage. In the palid light she saw him eye it hungrily and bury his face in the wilted thing. He took great famished bites of dirt, rot and cabbage.

"What'd I tell you, lady?" the driver boasted. "A sight, isn't it?" He flicked the reins, turned the bus and noisily they clattered over the cobblestone pavement toward a prettier part of the city.

Jane Addams didn't answer him. She could not speak. Her throat was so tight. To think that human beings were in such a sad state and she had never known! But now that she knew, what could she do—one woman, wearing a brace? Lights of beautiful London came into view as they crossed the Thames. Perhaps she could not do much, but she resolved to do something.

CHAPTER 5

❧ "BUT WHAT CAN I *DO?*" ❧

JANE ADDAMS FOUND that it is one thing to decide, in an exalted moment, to help the world—and quite a different thing to know how and where to begin. Others, before her time and since, have been confronted by this same practical problem and so have lost the first glow of purpose.

When she awakened the next morning, a Sunday, she found that Mrs. Addams had plans for attending church and engagements to visit with friends. After that there was more sightseeing and visiting, and so weeks passed until the day arrived for them to go to France. The scene of that Saturday evening in London's East End never quite left Jane's mind though it got pushed back by trivial occupations.

But one change resulted. Jane's distress that evening prompted a new kind of sightseeing that Mrs. Addams never suspected. When she had time to herself, Jane hunted poor districts and while wandering up and down

44

shabby streets, she tried to find whether someone, some-where, was trying to help these people. She was a stranger so she never found what she searched for. Had she known where to go and whom to ask, she might have learned that in this summer of 1883 there were several people living near the London market place who were working for the very poor she had seen.

Some time before that Saturday evening when Jane was seeing urban poverty for the first time, a small group of university people had decided that they would try to find some way to help the less fortunate. Several of this group of educated people were students at Oxford University, and among them was a young man named Arnold Toynbee.

Arnold's father had the idea that working men should have better living conditions—a novel thought at that time. He had built model cottages—most other employers hardly knew where the men lived, or how. Mr. Toynbee gave some public talks about art and invited working people to come to his house and see his beautiful pictures—an unheard of thing at that time. His neighbors thought he was a queer man, but the visitors liked the pictures. After young Arnold had finished some science courses, his father had him give a few talks on what he had learned. The workers who came were interested and they liked young Arnold and asked for more talks about subjects he had studied. The words "democracy" and "brotherhood" were not so glibly used in the eighteen-eighties, but Mr. Toynbee and his son practiced these ideals without talking about them.

Young Arnold became interested in so many subjects that he had a hard time choosing a profession. Should he enter the army, or study law, or go into government service? He liked each one. But he finally decided that he would study history and philosophy; surely these would give him an understanding of life. He worked so hard with his entrance studies that he became ill; it was quite some time before he could go on with his education.

During this hard period, Arnold's religion was a real help to him. One of his student friends told another, "Arnold reads his Bible as though it was an ordinary book—he reads as though he likes it."

A person who is ill has plenty of time for thinking. Arnold found himself thinking a great deal about one certain verse: "Love thy neighbor as thyself." Just what did that mean? The general idea seemed good but how did a person start loving a neighbor? As Jane Addams was to discover, later, it was not easy to put that verse into everyday living.

When Arnold Toynbee was well enough to go to college, he decided he would make an experiment in a new kind of living. He rented a room near St. Jude's Church in the crowded part of East London, and he lived there during his vacations. The neighborhood was very different from his beautiful home, and his way of living changed. He joined a working man's club. He went to the Vicar of St. Jude's and offered to help in any way. He took his turn at speaking before his new club and because the members liked him, he was asked to talk again.

Very soon he saw that he did not know much about this awful condition called poverty that was all around him.

"It is not enough to be friendly to working people," he told a classmate when he went back to college. "If I want to help them, I must know more about what makes poverty. I am going to take some new courses." He had hated economics and political science but now that he had a good reason for taking them, he worked hard. After he graduated he wrote a history of the Industrial Revolution, explaining some of the problems of men and machines, and he made talks, to working people and to other groups. He had a tiny income from his family but he needed to earn most of his living, so he worked long hours.

People liked Arnold Toynbee. "That chap understands us," a workingman said to a friend. You ought to hear his lecture. He talks plain good sense."

But Jane Addams knew nothing of all this, then. She did not even know that Arnold Toynbee died in March of 1883—all his work, all his dreams seemingly wasted.

The grand tour, piloted by Mrs. Addams continued. They visited Holland, Germany, Austria, Italy, Greece and finally arrived in Paris. Jane studied languages in each country. She visited churches and art galleries. She went to concerts and slipped off when she could to see city slums. Her health was the best it had ever been but she was uneasy, dissatisfied and restless. The tour lasted twenty-two months and she was glad when it ended.

Jane Addams had corresponded with Ellen Starr ever since Ellen left Rockford Seminary at the end of her freshman year. The girls told each other everything with the greatest frankness. Now, from her home in Cedarville, Jane wrote thousands of words to Ellen, telling of her desires—and her uncertainties.

"I want to do something!" she wrote, "But what can one not very strong person do about poverty?"

"Poverty is everywhere," Ellen replied. "Get out and do something at home."

Jane did try, but the shabby houses that had shocked young Jane were so much better than the awful slums of Europe that she was not stirred. In Cedarville and Freeport there was sunshine, and space for little gardens. Schools were being opened; the towns were prosperous. East End, in London, was very different from Illinois, and East End haunted Jane.

She studied religion and joined the Presbyterian Church. That gave her comfort but it also increased her urge to work for her fellow men.

"I wish I had had a call to foreign missions as some of the girls at Rockford had," she wrote to Ellen. "They were fortunate; they knew what they wanted to do."

All the years since she left Rockford, Ellen had been teaching school—and saving every possible penny for travel abroad. Now the time had come and she sailed away. Jane's letters followed her and in writing these Jane Addams suddenly saw herself as Ellen must see her.

"Look at me," she said to herself one day, "I'm twenty-seven and healthier than I've ever been. I write articles for magazines and they are returned, every one of them. I stay with sister Mary and help mind her children. I manage my little inheritance and live on what father left me. But I do no work that amounts to anything. I'm a failure—and I don't like the sound of the word." She closed the letter, then chewed the end of her pen and thought of a score of possibilities, none of them to her liking.

"I shall go abroad and travel with Ellen," she announced a week later. "I'll go to Rome and study early Christianity, that ought to be a worthy subject." She persuaded a friend, Sarah Anderson, to go with her (that would appease her family) and in December of 1887 they met Ellen.

The winter in Rome turned out badly because Jane promptly got a serious form of rheumatism that laid her low until spring. She finally insisted that Ellen and Sarah go on with their travels in southern Italy.

In the spring Jane was well enough to join them in Spain. Perhaps it was the weeks of illness in Rome, perhaps the weariness of endless preparation for a task she could not even name, perhaps it was that the seed planted in her mind that Saturday evening in East End, London —whatever the reason, on an Easter Day in Spain, Jane Addams was through with dallying.

"I am sick of *us*!" she exclaimed to Ellen. "We travel around and look at sights. We study languages. We con-

template architecture. We view paintings. We don't *do* anything!"

"But what can we do?" Ellen asked, reasonably.

Jane stared at her, daunted by the question. Said aloud by another person, the phrase that had been running in her mind terrified her.

"What can I *do*? Ellen, I don't know. But I mean to find out. Tomorrow I shall start for America."

The next morning she and Ellen conferred. Jane told again her dream of a big house among little houses.

"I want my big house to be in Chicago. I wish you would come with me, Ellen. I shall need you. Together we could do much more than I can alone. Will you come?"

Ellen, her face white, said nothing for several minutes. The rattle of a passing cart, the plaintive cry of a beggar beneath the window were the only sounds in the quiet room in that Spanish inn.

"For a moment you surprised me, Jane," Ellen said softly. "But I'm not really surprised. I've known for a long time that you wanted this; that we must. . . ."

"*We!*" Jane exclaimed. "Oh Ellen, then you will!"

"Yes," Ellen answered. Her voice was natural now, and her color had come back. "I want to help. But we have much to learn, Jane—we have been wasting time. We have no idea how to go about starting a big house among little ones but I think I know where we can learn. When I was in London, before you came over I went to Toynbee house—didn't I write you about it?"

"U-um-m—tell me now," Jane said.

"There's a place in the East End called Toynbee Hall. It's named after a young man who died five years ago. He had ideas about people being friends with each other. They call the place a settlement house or a social settlement because people settle there, among the poor and are neighbors."

"What kind of people, Ellen?" Jane asked.

"Oh, college people, mostly. People who have studied too much, as maybe you and I have, and there they learn from their neighbors what life really is. They give and they take. The poor learn about art and books and music that they have had no time for and the others learn about people and life."

"A kind of mission, maybe?" Jane asked, fascinated. "I didn't know you knew all this, Ellen!"

"No, Toynbee Hall is not a mission." Ellen smiled at Jane's starry eyes. "A mission tries to change people. A settlement just wants to *know* people and then, if it is possible, help them to help each other. Perhaps they both change with the learning though the idea is not the changing, but the getting to be friends."

"It sounds perfect," Jane said rapturously. "I'm sick of studying and preparing and wondering what to do. We'll settle where the most people live and then we can learn."

"We ought to go to London," Ellen began planning. "We ought to talk with the Toynbee Hall residents. Sarah can go with us to Paris, she was to sail home next week anyway. We'll stay in London only long enough to get our bearings—then home.

"Can you pack in an hour, Jane?"

In London, Ellen and Jane visited Toynbee Hall and had many conferences with the Director. Samuel Barnett had known Arnold Toynbee and was carrying out the young man's ideal. His talk was sensible and straightforward.

"Every man has in him the power to make his life," Mr. Barnett remarked during one visit. "The greatest service you can do any man is to help him discover his own power and inspire him to use it. Your greatest chance for this comes if you are his friend."

They saw children of workingmen coming to Toyn-bee Hall for classes, for food, for comfort. They attended evening adult classes in art, music, reading, and they saw that weariness was forgotten when the students were truly interested.

"It's all like seeing a dream come true, Ellen," Jane said happily. "Abraham Lincoln would have liked this place —people working together like this gives each an equal chance. In Chicago we will have many races and more kinds of people than here—but this plan will work there, too. You'll see! We can try *living* Christianity."

"We shall need to know bookkeeping," said practical Ellen. "Mr. Barnett reminded me of that this morning."

"Well, then, I'll learn bookkeeping," Jane agreed. "But we must not stay here longer. I want to begin work."

CHAPTER 6

❧ THE SEARCH ❧

JANE AND ELLEN AR-
rived home in June
of 1888. They were enthusiastic about their "big house,"
and they meant to find it immediately. But first, Jane
must study her modest investments; she was to pay all
expenses. These business matters made her remember
that course in bookkeeping that she had promised to take.
It took time, but was necessary; their new life must be
well managed.

Of all Jane's family, only sister Mary was interested
in her plans for a "big house." The others thought she
had silly notions and tried to dissuade her. Jane went to
visit Mary—and stayed weeks nursing sick nephews. So
the storms of January had buried Chicago deep in snow
when Jane Addams arrived to begin her search for a
neighborhood and a house.

Chicago in the eighteen-eighties was an amazing city.
It had a population of 1,099,850 and about three-fourths
of these were foreign-born or children of foreign-born

parents. Italians, Germans, Irish, Polish, Scandinavians, Austrians, Russians and others had come to the Middle West. Thousands of these had settled in Chicago; they called it the "Gateway to Opportunity." Because new arrivals did not speak English, they usually went directly to a neighborhood where earlier immigrants from the same nation had already settled. There were many practical reasons for this and no disrespect to the new country or its language was intended. The newcomers loved America—they seldom used the full name, the United States of America, and likely did not understand the reason for the longer name. They came with high hopes and wanted to be citizens as soon as possible. But a new arrival needed time to pick up American ways as well as the new language.

So whole sections of Chicago became foreign cities inside an American city. A foreign tongue was spoken on the streets and in shops which catered to foreign tastes. Foreign-language newspapers flourished and church services were in native tongues. Jane Addams visited many such communities trying to decide where to settle. Because she was a stranger in the city, she sought the help of newspapermen, real estate agents and anyone who would aid in her search. The quest seemed endless; she never even glimpsed the place of her dreams. But she did begin to know Chicago.

Halsted Street fascinated her. It is about thirty-two miles long and was said to be the longest straight street in the world. A middle section of about six miles, from the river shipyards to the stockyards, went through several "foreign colonies." Between Halsted and State Streets, a mile to the east, thousands of Italians were crowded together. Nearby, on side streets, were Poles and Russians, and a big Irish section was just south. Bohemians lived a little southwest, down Blue Island Avenue around Eighteenth and Central Streets. Jane Addams usually turned down that avenue on her exploring and was quickly in "Little Pilsen," the third largest Bohemian "city" in the world. Going west on Eighteenth one abruptly left the poor neighborhoods and came upon Ashland Avenue, a mile west of Halsted, which was the fashionable street of the well-to-do. That amazing mixture was typical of Chicago.

Ellen Starr, meanwhile, had a living to earn. She had resumed her work of teaching in a fashionable northside school in Chicago. But after school, Jane often rented a horse and buggy and together the friends explored. They saw narrow, filthy streets; garbage piled high in wooden boxes; alleys, mere dirty lanes, and stables that stank, even in the cold weather.

Jane and Ellen saw people as gaunt and weary as those who had stirred Jane in London, but with one marked difference, London's poor were almost all British—Chicago's poor were of every race and creed. They saw many who had gathered oranges in Calabria and olives in Greece. Women who had gleaned wheat in the poppy-bright fields of Europe or dug peat in the bogs of Ireland. And in these faces Jane thought she saw a hunger for something more than food. It spurred her to search daily for her house.

Of course she saw hundreds of houses. Mostly they were one-story or story-and-a-half cottages built for one family and now lived in by four or more families. Often shacks had been hurriedly erected in tiny back yards for two families more. Few had sewer connections. A pump, or perhaps one water pipe in the back yard and one out-house served all the people on the lot.

Chicago's population had more than doubled in the ten years preceding this spring. There literally had been no time to properly house the floods of eager, hopeful people who poured into the city. Jane saw thousands of little houses—but where was a big house? She could not find it.

One Sunday afternoon, Jane was taken to a meeting in the Bohemian neighborhood. She was busy talking with her friends in the carriage, but because it had become a habit, she glanced at buildings. When she returned to her lodging that evening Ellen came for a brief call.

"Do you know, Ellen," Jane said, "I think maybe I saw our house today. I didn't notice it till we had passed —but I think it is the very place I want. A big brick house with white pillars and porches and—"

"It certainly sounds like nothing we have seen!" Ellen laughed. "And it's not like you to indulge in wishful thinking."

"Nor am I," Jane insisted, half vexed. "I'll take you to it tomorrow—you'll see."

As soon as Ellen could leave school they set out in the hired buggy.

"It was a Bohemian meeting, so of course we went down Blue Island Avenue," Jane explained as she turned the corner. "Then it wasn't very far . . ."

She drove slowly and they watched every building. But they found no place with white pillars and porches. Annoyed, Jane turned back and they searched again. They went up and down side streets, narrow passage-ways teaming with children, pushcarts, and stray dogs. But they did not find the house. Darkness came and they had to turn toward home. But Jane went on hunting that house. She was too shy to ask anyone about it—it was silly to say to these helpful people, "I saw a house and now it isn't where I thought it was!" What would they think of her? She could find it herself.

Spring came and on a sunny day the architect, Allen Pond, drove Jane to see a certain neighborhood near the Bohemian section; he thought it might interest her. They started down Halsted Street.

"Shouldn't we turn here?" Jane asked Mr. Pond when he drove by Blue Island Avenue. "That's the way we always go."

"Well, perhaps it is the better way," Mr. Pond said politely. "We can turn at Polk Street—it's only a couple of blocks further south."

As they neared the corner, Jane cried out and clutched his arm.

"Oh, stop, Mr. Pond! There's my house!" Jane was in

a dither of excitement.

"That place!" Mr. Pond was astonished at her excitement. "That's the Hull mansion. It's been right there for thirty-three years."

"Well, Ellen and I have been searching for it these many weeks," Jane told him, marveling. "We always turned off at the Avenue—serves me right for being too sure.

"That's the place I want to live in. It's perfect. Can we get it?"

Mr. Pond guided his horse toward the gutter so that the stream of horse-drawn trucks, mule-drawn wagons, push-carts, and people could flow by them. Then they sat, studying that brick house.

"I doubt if this is what you want, Miss Addams," he said regretfully. He hated to dampen her enthusiasm. "This was once a good house. I recall looking it up about a month ago when the owner, Charles J. Hull, died. It was built in 1856 for his own residence and it was a handsome place in its day."

"It's a fine house now," Jane retorted briskly. "I could move in this hour."

"But you'll not have the chance," Mr. Pond said, disturbed by her assurance. "The property is willed to Mr. Hull's cousin, a Miss Helen Culver—Hull's wife and children died before him. And it is occupied. South of of the center hall you can see a saloon. The north half looks like a furniture storage place and upstairs, tenement rooms, let out to many families. Of course the

Hulls moved away years ago. A pity to see a nice place
go down. In its day grass was green under those old oaks
and there was a garden. Hull built it as his suburban residence. A mile south of Madison Street seemed a long
way out in that day."

Jane Addams sat quietly, now, studying the house, admiring its really fine lines. Upstairs were four big rooms
or perhaps six smaller ones and a central hall with little
rooms at each end, front and back. The windows were
rounded at the top, and a wide porch supported by white
pillars went entirely around the building. It had fallen
into shabby ways but it was still sound, she guessed.
Later she learned that only by a whiff, a breeze had
saved it from the great fire of '71 which started in a nearby stable.

"That is the place I have been searching for," Jane
said to Mr. Pond. "Will you help me get possession? It
has everything I want—the crowded foreign neighborhood, the dirt, the hunger I see on tired faces, hunger for
more than food. I can make this a real home. Please help
me—I can't wait longer."

Mr. Pond promised to act quickly.

Late that same afternoon, Jane brought Ellen to see
the house. Already the way seemed familiar to her, she
was going home. They drew the buggy to the side of the
street and studied the house lovingly.

"I can hardly believe we have found it," Jane said
almost reverently. "It's exactly the building I have seen
in my dreams ever since that long ago day when father

drove me near the mill in Freeport."

"See the wonderful neighbors we shall have," Ellen whispered. "Irish, Assyrian, German, Bohemian—that old woman over there is surely Austrian and that child is a Pole. We must get it, Jane!"

"*Get it!*" Jane exclaimed. "Of course we'll get it! Think I would lose it now that I have found it?"

Fortunately Miss Culver was interested in what Mr. Pond told her of Miss Addams's plans, and an interview was arranged.

"I could not let you have the whole building at," Miss Culver told Jane, after they had talked a while. "There are some leases. . ." Jane waited anxiously, but her faith never wavered. "If you don't mind starting with a part of the house, I could let you have the hall, the south rooms and the second floor very soon. Then later, the furniture in storage can be moved and you may use the whole building."

"You are very good," Jane said humbly. Words were inadequate to express the gratitude she felt. "You trust a stranger, a stranger with a dream."

Helen Culver smiled. "I, too, have a dream. My cousin Charles made most of his fortune in Chicago. He had a gift, as Mr. Pond may recall, for recognizing good property and he bought and sold as the city grew. He had the novel idea, too, of building workingmen's cottages and selling it to the tenants, taking payment in small installments. His concern about housing prompted him to do this work, but in the end it added to his fortune. Now that he is dead, I mean to return to Chicago money that he made here. Perhaps your plan for this neighborhood is the very project I am looking for—who knows?"

By midsummer the legal matters were settled and Jane and Ellen went to work on the house. Jane's sister, Mary Linn, sent her friend Mary Keyser to help them and the three scrubbed and painted and washed windows.

"What are we going to call this place, Jane?" Ellen Starr asked as they worked.

"I've been thinking about that," Jane answered. "The neighborhood is used to the name of Hull. I think we should name it 'Hull-House'—it seems to fit."

"Hull-House," Ellen said the words thoughtfully. "Why, that's what I have already called it, not thinking of the words as a name."

"You see?" Jane said gaily. "It named itself! Hull-House it shall be."

Finally the house was clean and ready, and Jane began the delightful task of furnishing. No young bride ever went at this business with greater enjoyment. She brought choice pieces of family mahogany from Cedarville. She hung her precious pictures, brought from Europe and framed to fit these wall spaces. The high ceilinged rooms, the handsome marble mantel, the graceful moldings all lent themselves to the elegant furnishings and by the time she had added new and carefully selected chairs, sofas and tables it looked charming. Silver, china, linen—and the place became a home.

All this activity, the moving out of former tenants, the cleaning and painting, the moving in, had, of course, been carefully watched by the whole neighborhood. The three newcomers often overheard frank comments as they went in or out.

"They surely have a lot of pictures," one young woman remarked. "I just wish my Tony could have seen the one she took in then—Rome, it was, I'm certain. Though it might have made him homesick, no telling." The words were spoken in Italian. Mary Keyser did not understand them. But Jane, walking with her, understood, and thought gleefully that now she was rewarded for her months of studying Italian.

Jane smiled, and, speaking in Italian, invited the young woman to come and bring Tony to see the pictures tomorrow. The young woman stared. A woman in Chicago speaking *Italian*! She could hardly believe her ears. A woman who drove a horse and buggy inviting her, Magda, to call. Magda didn't know that the vehicle was merely rented!

The next day, September 18, 1889, the three friends moved in. That evening they were to have supper in Hull-House. The search had ended. The dream now had shape in brick and wood. But a bigger problem lay ahead. Would the neighbors come to see them, as Jane expected? It wouldn't be long, now, until they knew.

CHAPTER 7

❧ THE NEW NEIGHBORS ❧

THE NEXT MORNING came and passed—and the doorbell did not ring. The three residents washed dishes, hung curtains and pictures, dusted and carried out papers and boxes. Mary Keyser was the housekeeper but, as the place was large—all the upstairs and more than half the first floor—the others had promised to lend a willing hand.

Near noontime, Mary went to market and she felt the curious stares that followed her down the block. The grocer filled her order and packed the food into her basket. But as she left, his curiosity got the better of him.

"What's the reason you folks have come here to live?" he asked bluntly.

Jane had warned Mary that they might be asked this— she was ready for him.

"We like Hull-House," she replied, smiling. "We like this neighborhood. Why do you live here, yourself?"

"'Cause I can't afford better," he said crossly. "I'm

telling you—that's the only reason anyone lives on this filthy street. And why the likes of you come here I don't see! You've got nice things. There's somethin' queer, that I know." The words tumbled out angrily. With the sensitiveness of the very poor, he feared, vaguely, for himself and his neighbors. Were these kindly-looking women making fun of them?

"Nothing queer at all," Mary replied in a matter of fact tone as she shifted her basket to her left arm. "And Mr. O'Malley, I do hope some of the ladies will call upon us. Once we are settled, now, we'll be getting lonesome without friends nearby." He stared at her, speechless, as she walked away.

As it happened, their first visitor came that afternoon and she was not Irish or German or Italian, but a pleasant young Englishwoman.

"Mother thought I should run in and call. I hope I am not being bold," she explained timidly when Miss Addams answered the doorbell. "No, I'll not come in. You are busy. We just wanted you to know that it seems good to see you here. We can't get used to America. We never guessed it was all so *foreign*!"

"Do come in and have tea with us," Jane said. "Mary has just put the kettle on, and we are through with work for the day." She led the way into the back parlor and introduced Ellen and Mary. "Aren't we lucky to have a visitor the first day!"

Over the teacups the English girl told their story. She and her widowed mother had come to America to be near relatives but when they arrived, they found her uncle had died and the family had moved away with no address left behind. The two women had had to get along alone. They had never earned a living; they had never lived in a city, and almost all their money had been spent for the journey. They had to begin at the very bottom—scrubbing floors by night in office buildings. They found rooms in the cheapest tenements and saved thriftily, hoping to move into better quarters. But getting ahead was slow, painful business.

The Hull-House people listened with eager interest.

"You don't know how glad mother will be to know that you speak English." The girl ended her story—"May I bring her to call?"

"Come whenever you can, both of you," Jane Addams said. "And I shall call upon your mother some late afternoon. Would that be the best time?"

Smiling and cheerful, the visitor left after promising to come again.

The next morning a timid knock on the door sent Jane Addams dashing, breakfast napkin still in her hand. Why had anyone knocked when the doorbell was in plain sight? She flung open the door and there stood a pretty, young Italian mother, a baby in arms and a three-year-old hanging to her skirt.

"I don't know what to do!" she said anxiously, in Italian. "I daren't leave the children alone. The friend who usually stays with them is awfully sick and if I'm late I'll lose my job! Mr. O'Malley says you are kind ladies—could you mind the babies while I hunt someone to stay with them—could you?"

"Oh, we'll be glad to keep them all day!" Miss Addams cried. Already she had reached for the hand of the three-year-old. Mary Keyser came running to take the baby. "The three of us will be here all day. We'll like the children for company. Don't you worry a minute!"

"They've had no breakfast yet—I was so worried—" the young mother said shyly. The fragrance of coffee and bacon was unmistakable. Surely this was a nice place and the ladies, very understanding of her plight.

"Come in, my dear," Ellen Starr said. "There is plenty for us all!"

"That's kind of you, I must hurry. But I know the children are hungry. Nita, you eat nicely," she told the little girl. "I've not had much chance to train her. My husband was killed in the factory where he worked and we had nothing laid by yet," she explained eagerly. "We've not been over long." The clock in the hall began to tick. "Oh, I'll have to run—I'll be late!" And she dashed down the steps.

The next morning the same two children arrived for the day and a Polish mother brought in three more, all under four years old. By good luck one of Ellen Starr's North Side friends was Jenny Dow, a pretty and intelligent young girl who was not satisfied with days of parties and gaiety. At Ellen's invitation, Jenny came to see the five children—and she stayed to help with them.

That was the beginning of Hull-House kindergarten for the children of working mothers. Jenny was a great help at Hull-House. She was well educated and eager for work, and she entered into the spirit of the house from that first day. Her kindergarten became a joy for the mothers and children and an education for the three residents. They were astonished to find degrees of social distinction even among families of the same nationality and equal poverty.

Small Toni came, each morning, with what appeared to be the same grime that Jenny had soaped from his face the day before. Tenement dwellers had to carry cold water from the pipe in the yard to the upper floors; fuel for heating was too costly to waste, no wonder most of the children were dirty! But just the same, Toni drew himself away from pretty, and equally grimy, Angelina.

"I don't want to sit by *her*!" he announced to Jenny.

"She eats her macaroni wrong—see?"

Jenny watched as Angelina, at mid-morning lunch, tipped her head back and dropped into her open mouth this food that she liked best.

"Now let me see *you* eat," Jenny said, her eyes dancing impishly.

Proudly Toni cut the long macaroni with his fork and lifted it into his mouth. "We eat this way, at *our* house," he said. "This is the *right* way."

Angelina smiled at him adoringly, apparently recognizing his superiority. Already she knew that he was gentry and she only a peasant. She had no resentment; she was too young to care—yet.

Jenny moved Angelina to the other end of the table. And that evening, before she went home, she reported the incident to the residents.

"Table manners are always a badge of social distinction," Ellen Starr agreed.

"Then we should be particular to teach these littlest ones the best manners," Jane Addams said thoughtfully. "In time that may mean as much to them as the actual food we give them. It may help them to raise their standards all along the line. I'd not thought of it before, Jenny. I think you have found something important, here."

"Important," Ellen repeated, "because it is so trivial we might never have discovered it. The so-called little things keep people apart. Here at Hull-House let's teach what will bring them together. Table manners will be the beginning."

For several years Jenny Dow came daily to be with the children. On her last day, when she was leaving to be married, she found that all this time the children had thought that she was a little girl, dressed up for play in a great white apron. Even when she told them about her wedding, they could hardly believe that she was a grownup!

Most of Jenny's work was for children. Not all, though —there was the old woman and the hole in the wall. In Jenny's first month of service, Jane Addams answered the doorbell and greeted a woman who wept so bitterly she could hardly speak.

"We've got to move again," the woman sobbed, "and no one will have us!"

"Tell me about it," Jane Addams said, drawing her indoors away from the curious who flocked so quickly at a sign of woe.

"It's my old grandmother!" she cried. "The old thing is passed ninety and can't get from her bed, she's that weak. We have to leave her alone all day—how else can we earn a living? If one of us stayed for company, there'd not be enough to eat, I'm telling you."

"I expect she is lonely," Jane suggested, puzzled. "Would you like us to call and see her?"

"Thanks," the woman said briefly, "but it's worse than lonely she is." Vexation dried the tears and she spoke bitterly. "All day, while we are gone, she picks at the plaster —every inch of the plaster her fingers can reach—and the room is too small to move the bed away from the wall. Her fingers keep at it and now word has got around. This landlord orders us out and no other will take us! What we'll do—that I'm not knowing!"

"She's lonely," Jane Addams began, compassionately. But Jenny, passing along the hall, had heard.

"The poor thing wants something for her fingers to do," Jenny exclaimed. "Plaster is interesting. I used to pull it off myself when I was a child, till I got my fingers slapped! I can't leave the children just now. But if you will show Miss Addams where you live, I'll come over soon and see your grandmother. And I'll think of something for those fingers. Jane, can you help with finding them a house? I'll promise Grandmother pulls no more plaster!"

Later that day Jenny set out with a basket. Soon she pulled up a stool by the tumbled bed and unpacked bright-colored papers, blunt-end scissors and a jar of paste. The old woman was entranced.

"For me!" she exclaimed. "Those pretties?"

"All for you," Jenny agreed. "And we are going to make trimmings for your room." They set to work, Jenny showing how paper strips could be pasted to make links that gradually grew into long chains. They finished one and Jenny fastened it to the wall with tiny pins.

"Tomorrow I shall come again at this same time," Jenny said, when the gay decoration had been properly admired. "I shall expect to hang *two* chains—you'll have to work hard to have them ready for me."

The wizened face glowed. Grandmother had no words for her joy.

"I'll try to find some plaster," Jenny went on casually. "I think we'd better cover up that hole before I hang the chains—would you like that?"

The old woman nodded, tears rolling down her face. Jenny mended the plaster. The landlord, brought by Miss Addams to see what was being done, allowed the family to stay on, and Jenny kept the eager fingers busy as long as the grandmother lived.

As word of the Hull-House residents and their odd but friendly ways spread around, neighbors came to call. Jane and Ellen returned each visit promptly; they never forced themselves but they responded to every gesture of friendliness—or of curiosity that might grow into friendship.

That fall they invited their first Italian visitor and one of her friends to come for supper and stay to see their photographs of Italy. The visitors helped "do dishes" and then the pictures were spread out on the table.

"Oh! My mother would love to see this one!" the younger girl exclaimed. "Mother was born there—in that cottage. We lived just beyond that turn in the road. May she see these?"

"Bring her next Thursday," Miss Addams said. "And if you have friends from your village, bring them, too."

That was the beginning of a young woman's club that soon was meeting once a week. The residents invited two guests each week, for supper, and to "clear." Promptly afterward the room filled with eager Italians, homesick for a sight of loved scenes.

Looking backward, after a few months, it seemed that the use of Hull-House increased with astonishing speed. Soon there were clubs for girls, for boys, for young adults. Jane Addams's days were crowded with work that she loved. And soon she was invited beyond the neighborhood of Polk and Halsted Streets, for the work widened as it grew.

CHAPTER 8

∾ HULL-HOUSE A MAGNET ∾

ON THE SIXTH OF OCTO-
ber, a friend sent Jane
Addams a dozen red roses to celebrate her first birthday
in Hull-House. Jane always enjoyed a gift more when
she shared it, so she promptly re-wrapped the lovely
flowers and carried them to an invalid Italian neighbor,
the mother of one of Jenny's kindergarten children.

"Oh, the lovely things!" the mother exclaimed. Then
she held them away, studying their beauty. "I can't believe they are so fresh! It's like magic that they kept so
well, all the long journey. Three weeks it takes from
Italy and these are as fresh as though just cut!"

"These are not from Italy," Miss Addams said, in surprise. "These grew in Chicago."

"Don't pretend to me!" the patient laughed with good
humor. "I ought to know! I've lived in Chicago for ten
years and never a rose—never any bloom have I seen.
They don't have flowers in America. I know and I miss
my little garden."

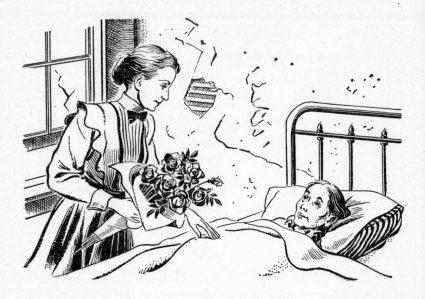

What could Jane Addams say? The woman had no idea that a mile away florists' windows were gay with bloom the year around. She did not know that in summer a five-cent carfare would take her to the big blue lake, passing scores of gardens on the way. No American had taken the trouble to know the stranger or to invite her to see other parts of the city.

"It is time there was a Hull-House," Jane Addams said when she recounted the incident at supper. The next time she spoke in a North Side drawing-room she re-told the story of her roses and it aroused more interest than talk about sociological theories.

After that, she told more of personal incidents in her talks. But she was careful to take a neighbor with her— "to keep me from over-dramatizing," she told Ellen. Not even for a cause would she forget the lesson of exact truth that her father had taught her.

Helen Culver, the owner of Hull-House, was pleased with the way Hull-House work grew. Soon she got the stored furniture out and gave the residents the use of the whole house. Later she gave Jane Addams a five-year lease of the place, for a nominal dollar a year rental. Eventually Hull-House was incorporated so that it could legally accept the gift of the property and other gifts, and could administer its finances. With Miss Culver's generous assistance, Hull-House grew faster in size and wider in scope of service than would otherwise have been possible. The cooperation of Jane Addams and Helen Culver was a wonderful thing for Chicago and made a pattern which was followed in other cities.

That corner was a crossroad of many nationalities. Hull-House quickly came to be a kind of magnet that drew men, women and children to its door. Visitors were the sick, the lonely, the needy, the scoffers and the curious. All were kindly received. All were freely shown through the house, though before the winter was over that task came to be a wearisome chore.

Visitors whispered frank comments, not too quietly sometimes, little guessing that their native tongue, German, Italian or Greek, was understood.

"These women must be cracked, living here alone!"

"The place is clean now—but just wait! Soon it will be dirty like other houses and then who will scrub—and them all ladies!" (Of course the scrubbing was done by

Mary and Jane and Ellen, after the visitors had departed.)

Other comments were inspiring to the residents.

"Look at those pictures, they're pretty. See that one, sister, it's like grandmother's village in Sicily!"

"Look at their ceiling, Mother! We've seen nothing so pretty since we came to America!"

Visitors came, too, from other parts of Chicago and went away pondering. This year, the beginning of the eighteen-nineties, was a period of great change in America, especially in the cities. Thousands of new immigrants were arriving at Ellis Island and other ports, attracted by rumors of work and of high wages. But, unknown to them, the period of greatest railroad and canal building was drawing to a close. The time of free grants of land was about over, and machines were taking the place of men in industry.

Not knowing or understanding this, the immigrants poured into cities where their only chance to earn a living was unskilled labor. Thousands who could not speak a word of English and lacked the "know-how" that might have helped them to better jobs, crowded into cheap, shabby tenements and wondered how they were to find the America of their dreams.

At this time the profession of Social Work was almost unknown. Few people had any idea what a "Settlement" was. But many were thinking about social responsibility and wishing they knew something to do about this vast thing—a city. As Jane Addams went about, telling of her new home, she made friends for Hull-House. Her speaking had improved since the day when she failed to win the state contest for Rockford. She spoke in a low, clear voice. Her phrases varied from time to time but always she explained what Hull-House hoped to be.

"We borrow the word 'Settlement' from London," she said to her audiences, and then she told the story of Arnold Toynbee and the house that was named for him. "But really, the idea of a settlement is as American as it is English, for our pioneers went from one place to settle in another, just as Ellen and I have chosen to 'settle' on Halsted Street.

"We at Hull-House hope to give opportunity to your young people who wish to learn the best ways of helping their fellowmen of every race and creed. If we do not give young leaders a practical, definite way of expressing their ideals they may continue studying too long, as I did. They may be shut away from common labor, miserable because they do not know how to live their ideal of democracy.

"The world grows better because people wish that it should and take steps to make it better. Progress depends on change . . . someone must be willing to take the first steps . . . must learn to know life as it is, both the good and the evil. . . .

"What good does it do for *some* of us to enjoy the arts, painting, music and literature if thousands around us hunger for beauty? The benefits of civilization to be permanent must be universal!"

After her talks, people always plied her with questions and comments.

"Surely, Miss Addams," someone was certain to say, "you don't expect to abolish slums and poverty by living with them? The Bible admits that the poor are always with us. What can you hope to do against such odds?"

"We can be friends and neighbors," she replied, with quiet dignity. "They can teach us what life really is. We can learn where our boasted civilization fails."

"And what then?"

"Perhaps in time Hull-House can be a sort of sign-post to show men how to live together in friendship—men could, you know, if enough people would take the trouble to understand each other." That word "understand" as she said it, was different from the colder word "tolerance" that some were using, often to cover a chill indifference. Tolerance—but who wants to be tolerated? Human beings crave understanding.

Her talks attracted to Hull-House many who, like the three who resided there, wanted to learn and to do something about their new knowledge.

Jenny Dow brought her friend Mary Rozet Smith to visit and Mary came daily to learn and to serve. She, like Jenny, had attended Kirkland School and knew Ellen Starr. She was a woman of wealth and culture, deeply interested in music. Mary Smith had traveled in countries that were "home" to Hull-House neighbors and she could speak many languages. She had a gift for discovering talented children and helping to educate them. It

was Mary Smith who organized the early Music Clubs
and worked long days training girls and boys for the concerts that packed Hull-House. Mary interested her father
in giving generously, and though she was never a resident, she gave money and service all the days of her life.

Julia Lathrop and Florence Kelley and Dr. Alice
Hamilton came to Hull-House as residents and their
interest in children, in housing, and in public health
widened the settlement's service.

Miss Lathrop had attended Rockford Seminary and
was graduated from Vassar in 1880, whereupon she
shocked her family by studying law. She was a vivid,
earnest woman, with dark eyes, piled-up dark hair and
keen wit—a wonderful companion. The Halsted Street
neighborhood needed her legal knowledge and took to
her at once. She had a gift for listening and then quickly,
and with a light, sure touch, coming to a decision. She
was appointed official visitor for Cook County's poor and
was a member of the State Board of Charities. (The first
resident of Hull-House to have a state job.) She also
had much to do with establishing the Juvenile Court in
Cook County, the first juvenile court in the nation. Miss
Lathrop lived at Hull-House until she went to Washington, as the first head of the new Federal Children's
Bureau.

Florence Kelley was of a Philadelphia Quaker family
and had been educated at Cornell University. She, too,
had traveled and spoke many languages. Miss Kelley was
interested in labor conditions—specially in sweat-shops

(a name given to airless rooms that could be rented cheaply for the making of clothing). Sweat-shops were stifling in summer, cold in winter, and dirty all the year. Clothing made in them was worn by the rich and the middle-income people who had no idea where their garments were made—not until an epidemic and Florence Kelley told them. Her work for factory inspection and decent working conditions resulted in the organization of the National Consumers' League and in some improvements in conditions of child labor.

Dr. Alice Hamilton came to Hull-House some time later than the others. She had attended Farmington, a finishing school, taken her medical degree at the University of Michigan and then studied at Johns Hopkins. She was a slender, attractive woman with grace of manner, and she worked tirelessly, teaching in medical college and doing research at Rush medical laboratories. Yet every day she shared the work at Hull-House, carried on medical studies in the neighborhood and treated the old people and the babies. Saturday mornings were set aside for scrubbing babies in the Hull-House basement —sessions of practical teaching for mothers. Dr. Hamilton made these mornings fun for everyone. She stayed at Hull-House until she was appointed professor of industrial medicine at Harvard in 1919.

And there were others, fifteen in all, a few men but more women in those early years, who came to live at Hull-House. None of them expected to re-make the world—they were not so foolish. But they did believe that if one took the trouble to understand people, good might come.

Perhaps the best known helper at Hull-House was never a resident. She lived in the city and was a member of one of Chicago's wealthy families. Mr. de Koven, her father, was so fashionable that he would not allow his daughter Louise to appear on the platform at school, when she was graduated.

"It is not fitting for a young woman of sixteen to appear in public!" he decreed. Nor would he allow her essay on "The Problems of the Working Man" to be read on that occasion.

Louise de Koven, however, proved to be a hard person to subdue. She decided to teach in Sunday school and was given a class of boys her own age. Promptly one of the boys defied her. She grabbed the rebel by the ears and dragged him outside the schoolroom. The boys' astonishment, she later admitted, more than her own strength, allowed her to reach the door. But she had no further behavior problems with that class.

Louise was a young matron, the wife of Joseph T. Bowen, one of Chicago's leading citizens, when she first heard of Jane Addams. By 1893, her curiosity brought her to Hull-House to visit, and ever after she was a godmother to the neighborhood.

One day Mrs. Bowen attended the new Hull-House Woman's Club, and because she was a visitor she was appealed to for advice about how to make a motion.

"I don't know anything about rules of order," she confessed frankly. "But I can learn. I'll look it up and tell you next time." After that she studied hard to keep ahead of their questions, and next thing she knew, she had been elected their president.

After a few meetings she suddenly decided that she was too well dressed. She took to wearing very plain, dark clothes when she came to Hull-House.

"You don't like us well enough to wear your pretty dresses any more," one member complained frankly.

"Oh, but I—I—" Mrs. Bowen paused. For once she did not know what to say.

"We liked to see our president smartly dressed," one of the other officers explained. "It is good for us. Makes us proud of our club." So after that Mrs. Bowen wore her best frocks to preside at the Hull-House Woman's Club.

The settlement became a kind of spiritual magnet attracting to the house at Halsted and Polk streets people of many talents. Inspired by Jane Addams, each new worker learned to know the neighbors and to serve them in some new way.

CHAPTER 9

❧ WORKING CHILDREN ❧

THE FIRST CHRISTMAS at Hull-House was to be celebrated with bright decorations, music and several parties, each planned for a different group. Already three music clubs—one for girls, one for boys and one for young adults—were practicing carols and the adults had learned a charming cantata to sing at their evening party.

Chicago people were generous at holiday-time. Many families made a practice of sending baskets of food to the poor, and since Hull-House was now becoming known, baskets began arriving there several days before the twenty-fifth.

"I wish we had some of these good things spread through the winter," Ellen Starr remarked when a dozen baskets arrived at one time, and busy people had to stop and attend to them. "Don't our friends know that people eat all the year around?"

"We'll have to use the perishables first," Jane Addams planned as she bustled about helping to unpack and sort the gifts. "A lot of this food will keep—look at all the canned goods! People mean to be generous, though many don't know how to go about it."

"A lot of this has come because of your talks on the North Side," Mary Keyser chuckled. "You make them want to do something—and giving food is what they think of first."

As Christmas Day came nearer, more gifts arrived— barrels of apples and potatoes, several turkeys, and candy. One candy factory sent several buckets of fine candy marked "For Christmas parties at Hull-House."

"When word of this gets around," Ellen Starr predicted, "we'll have more new members than the house will hold!"

"I remember how it was when I was a child," Mary Keyser agreed laughing. "We'd not miss a Sunday in December for we'd get a sack of candy for good attendance at Sunday School."

But to their surprise it did not seem to work out that way at Hull-House. Instead of increasing, the attendance at the girls' and boys' clubs dropped off; not half the regular number came to the Wednesday and Thursday meetings. The residents were puzzled.

"I'll find out about this," Jenny Dow said. "I have some young sisters in the kindergarten." The next morning she began asking questions.

"Ruth, where's your sister Naomi? She didn't come to Girls' Club yesterday."

Ruth sucked her fingers and look at the floor, uneasily.

"Is she sick?" Jenny persisted. Ruth shook her head.

"Has she gone visiting?" Jenny ventured wildly—though where the girl would visit she didn't know. Ruth shook her head again.

"Do you know where she is, Ruthie?" Jenny asked, really anxious now.

Ruth nodded, and two big tears rolled down her pale cheeks. "I'm not to tell," she whispered.

"Then never mind." Jenny decided that questions only worried the little girl. "She'll be back soon maybe?" Ruth brightened and ran to the kindergarten room.

That noon Jenny hunted up Miss Addams.

"There is *something* that is taking our children," she said. "If I had time, I'd go visiting—then I'd soon find out. But I can't leave today! Granny has sent a basket full of her paper chains and I promised to hang them before two so her granddaughter can fetch back the basket." She dashed off to her work. Miss Addams had appointments all day; Ellen Starr had to finish Christmas posters by herself, girls who had promised to help her had not come. So the mystery was left unsolved.

But on the twenty-third, the day of the girls' party, all the club members were there. Jane Addams thought several looked so weary that she wondered if they shouldn't really be at home in bed. What could ail them?

The party went off beautifully. The choruses sang like angels, Mary said. The children knew those loved carols so well that absence from rehearsals did not spoil the singing. They sat around the tree for the supper of sandwiches, cookies, and hot chocolate—and candy. Jenny Dow passed the candy.

Katie O'Reilly took one look at the plate of caramels before her—and was violently sick over everything! Jenny's helpers sprang to rescue the party, but more than half the children either declined the candy, or, much more distressing, were sick at the sight of it.

"What's the matter, Naomi?" Jenny Dow asked anxiously. Never before had she seen a party disintegrate so quickly. "Don't you like candy?" Naomi shook her head, *hard*.

Slowly, after the candy had been spirited away and the mess had been cleaned up, the story came out.

For six weeks those little girls had been working in a candy factory for fourteen hours each day, six days each week. Most of them were hired at a trifling wage, to wrap caramels. By way of safeguarding himself from theft the manufacturer had urged the girls to "eat all you want! Go ahead! Eat plenty!" The children were always hungry so their first day they ate caramels steadily—till they could hardly bear the sight of them. Yet daily they had wrapped caramels in a crowded, airless room; six weeks of that toil. No wonder they wanted none of those sweets at their party—for the candies Jenny passed them were from the very factory where these small girls had labored.

When the holidays had passed, the Hull-House residents decided to learn more about employed children. They had, of course, seen children who "helped mother"

as she "finished" clothing parceled out from clothing factories. But now, as they looked about, they saw that there was more child labor than they had suspected. Practically every family depended in part upon the children's earnings. Yet it was plain to an outsider that the children's health, as well as their education, was being damaged.

This toil was not forced on children by cruel parents who greedily exploited their sons and daughters! The truth was that the newly-arrived immigrant had a fearful struggle for existence. Often the additional pennies that the children could earn made the difference between eating and starving. And a bright boy or girl could get a job not open to a man. Parents honestly thought that their children *had* to work.

The immigrants were ambitious and eager to find the happiness that they had dreamed of in America. If they could just hang on till they learned the language and got a start . . . just for a time, they thought, and then life would be easier. As for the children, they expected to work. Had they not helped in the Old Country? They had fed the geese and gathered the feathers for beds. They had weeded garden and gleaned wheat from poppies by the fences; pounded flax and threshed oats. How could a family get along without the children's help?

But in this strange, crowded city there was no garden, no pond where the geese sported playfully, no sunny field to be gleaned. A family had to have *money*, something that the European peasant had had little need for except to pay his taxes and his journey to the new land.

From neighbors speaking the same language, or from her children, a mother might hear about work at "finishing" clothes. She probably counted herself lucky the day a neighbor brought a bundle of coarse suits such as workingmen wore. These must have buttons sewed on, buttonholes made and bastings removed. Naturally the mother called on her children to help. In winter they crowded around the stove; in summer they panted by the small window. Often they worked fifteen hours a day—but the pay was small, the whole family together earned about ten cents an hour.

The new social thinking about wages had hardly begun when Hull-House opened. Pay was forced down by women bidding against each other for needed work.

A working mother had no time to cook a tasty stew and the children discovered the delicatessen—which made more cash necessary. She could not nurse a sick child. And there was ever the terror that the father might be "laid off!" What could they do then?

Older boys and girls quickly picked up a few words of English and took on an American look. They got jobs in box factories or they pasted labels, or, if they were very lucky, they became "Cash" in a downtown store.

Department stores did not have the mechanical helps for completing a sale that afterward came into use. Instead they employed scores of girls and boys who ran to the cashier with the sales slip and the customer's money and brought back the change. Sometimes they carried the merchandise, too, and brought it back wrapped. As soon as a sale was made, the clerk shouted for the cash boy or girl. The bigger stores employed boys.

"Cash! *Cash!*" the salesperson called and the nearest "Cash" came on a run.

"Hurry now! Don't be idling on the way—the lady can't wait all day!" And off the "Cash" ran to the nearest cashier. "Cash" worked from seven in the morning till nine in the evening with twenty minutes for lunch—and no supper. Then there was the walk of a mile or two home before he could fall into bed.

In dull seasons children were dismissed from their jobs. Then they could go to school, if they still wanted to. Many did. There was real ambition in the neighborhood around Hull-House and the shifting population was in part due to families who learned new ways and language and moved to better sections. Night classes at Hull-House, advice of the residents and the comfort of knowing a neighbor who cared, put heart into many a family and helped them climb to better living.

The investigations of that first winter grew into careful surveys that the residents made public. These working children so appealed to Jane Addams that they drew her into politics, for she saw that help for them could come only through new laws. Largely because of the work of Jane Addams and other Hull-House residents, especially Mrs. Kelley and Miss Lathrop, Illinois passed its first child labor law in 1893. That was a tangible result they could view with pride.

Of course it was not enough to regulate children's hours

and working conditions. Miss Lathrop and Mrs. Bowen worked for a Juvenile Court, so needed to give first of-fenders and young children a fair chance when they had broken the law. It was a long uphill struggle and the Court was not finally established until 1899. But Julia Lathrop was its first officer and Mrs. Bowen its second.

All the while, Jane Addams thought about the families she knew. Her long years of European travel had not been wasted, as she once feared; they had fitted her to under-stand not only the languages but the homes her neighbors had left behind. She remembered the feeling of leisure in peasant homes. The whole family had long hours at hard toil for a meager living, but they never hurried as city people did. She remembered their tiny gardens where meals were eaten out of doors during many months of the year. She thought of the Greek athletic meets and the Italian religious festivals she had enjoyed. Most of these had been simple village gatherings but they had lifted the people out of their humdrum everyday living. In the city then there was nothing to take the place of these joys.

The immigrant had idealized America; for him it was opportunity. That was why he came, a new sort of pi-oneer. But the earlier American pioneer had had a true partnership with his wife. That did not seem possible in a city. In the old days a couple built a cabin together. Now the husband worked at a great distance—the wife hardly understood what he did, and there was little that they could enjoy together.

There was not even a place where a child, used to the

out-of-doors, could play in peace. Crowded rooms, a filthy back yard, streets thronged with teamsters shouting, horses and mules pulling loads—nowhere was there a safe place for play.

"How different it was when I was a child in Cedarville," Jane Addams remarked at supper after a day of neighborhood visiting. "George and I played in the mill, the orchard and the barn—it was all so fragrant and clean! We made collections and we had a place to keep them safely. Halsted street children have nothing like that—even their marks for hop-scotch are rubbed out quickly. And their housing—you should have seen where I went today!"

"*What* can *we* do?" the residents asked her. Indeed, she had no answer. Public playgrounds—they were unheard of. A living wage for men, and children required to attend school? No one even suggested it. Art and music and handwork in schools to give children more incentive to study? All such advantages were as yet dreams in the minds of a few.

But that first Christmas party and the children who sickened at the sight of candy started something that in time brought changes that were good for the nation as well as for the Halsted Street neighborhood.

CHAPTER 10

❧ THE LABOR MUSEUM ❧

C HRISTMAS HAD BEEN given over to the children, so Jane Addams decided that on New Year's Day grownups should have a party. The residents planned an "Open House" and boys and girls were told, "Bring your father and mother on New Year's Day!" "Bring your grandparents—we're having a party!" The day turned out to be one of the gayest they had known in the new home.

At that time, Bohemian and Italian families still wore their native costumes on special occasions, and on New Year's Day Hull-House rooms looked like a crossroad in Europe—because so many guests wore colorful clothes! Neighbors who were club members helped the resident hostesses; most of the guests had never been in the house before. The high ceilings, the marble mantel and, most of all, the pictures were much admired. Indeed, these pictures brought about the first addition to Hull-House. Ellen Starr had been having art classes and small exhibitions—but Hull-House was so crowded she had not room for all the work that she wanted to do. "If I only had a bigger place to hang these pictures," she often said, "they could be seen much better!" She interested a friend, Mr. Edward Butler, a successful Chicago merchant, and he gave the first large gift to Hull-House—money to build an art gallery.

Mr. Pond and his brother, who had helped put the Hull mansion into shape for Jane Addams, now designed the building for Mr. Butler. They put it on the south-east corner of the lot and built a covered passageway to connect it with the residence. The new Butler Gallery had a reading room on the first floor, an exhibition gallery and a studio above.

As word about Butler Gallery got around in Chicago many thought it strange that the first new building should be an art gallery—of all things!

"Aren't your neighbors poor?" Jane Addams and Ellen Starr were asked. "Don't they need something more practical than art?"

"People hunger for beauty as much as for food," was always their answer.

Still, the practical suggestion was worth trying. A Diet Kitchen was opened in the hope that working mothers would buy nourishing cooked food, sold at the lowest possible price. The kitchen did fairly well, but it was never the great success that the Butler Gallery continued to be. Jane Addams had put her finger on the greater need.

The evening the first exhibit opened in Butler Gallery crowds of people, most of them Italians, came to enjoy the pictures. Visitors stood before pictured scenes of their motherland, homesick tears in their eyes.

"I didn't know that Americans had pictures," a young man said to Miss Addams—in Italian of course.

"I thought Americans cared only for dollars," a shy Greek whispered. "I did not know anyone had pictures like these." He stood before photographs of Greek sculpture and felt a new bond, linking him with the country he had chosen.

In the new building there was room for the art and music and drama clubs. German evenings were soon as successful as the Italian evenings continued to be. One heard stirring Rhine songs; English classes rivaled drama nights in attendance. Miss Addams, ever thoughtful about bringing people together, invited an Evanston Drama Club to give, at Hull-House, a play they had presented in the North Shore suburb. The play was given in German and the Hull-House guests stamped and shouted their approval. During the dramatic third act several guests actually rolled on the floor in loud, enthusiastic laughter. It was very successful and the visitors departed well pleased.

But on the way home one Evanstonian began to wonder, "What do you suppose they really were laughing at," he asked. "Was our acting so wonderful? Or was our German pronunciation so bad? Perhaps we shall never know."

Jane Addams thought that the best thing Hull-House did was to furnish a place for neighbors to know each other. Under her roof, all were Americans. They saw that people who spoke another language were none the less neighbors with similar problems and joys. They learned to know each other and to speak a common language. Sometimes families asked Jane and Ellen to their homes, in a return hospitality. One or the other always accepted and felt it a privilege to be a guest.

Jane Addams never forgot the evening she first partook of the Passover Feast with Jewish friends who lived on a narrow, side street. The Jewish mother had taken traditional pains in preparing the food; she had chosen the meat and the manner of its slaughtering. She had followed Mosaic law about utensils in every detail. The evening was solemn and beautiful—a revelation to the visitor.

As she walked home, Jane Addams thought of her travels and of all the many mothers she had seen caring for their families in Europe. She remembered the Italian woman who kneels by the creek to wash the family garments. The Greek mother who patiently teaches her son to play the cithara, a kind of zither, so he can play for the festival. She thought of the Moorish woman who carries water on her head from the village well and the Scandinavian who bakes and brews, spins and weaves. How strange an American city must seem to them! There should be some sort of bridge, she thought, between the old life and the new. Between the mothers and the children who quickly took up with new ways. She talked about this when she arrived home.

"You expect too much of people," Ellen said. "There is always a gap between generations. The elders have experience; the young ones, the dreams. That's natural."

"But here the gap is too, too wide," Jane insisted. "Did you notice Toni last evening? He looked scornfully at his father when he asked me a question in Italian. Toni already prides himself on forgetting Italian! He shrugged his shoulders when I asked if his mother was well."

"That Toni!" Ellen chuckled. "He's a live wire! He gives his pay envelope to his father—now. But he is getting independent. One of these days he'll have a better job and he'll move his whole family to another part of town. He's getting Americanized fast."

"Yes, Toni is smart," Jane agreed smiling. "And I grant that some friction between old and young helps both. But here, I see too much. The young learn fast. The fathers work at a distance, they pick up new ways, though more slowly. But the mothers—how can a woman keep up with them when she stays at home sewing or scrubs floors all night and keeps house, after a fashion, all day? Naturally, she is tired and cross—I don't *blame* the children! But I think we should do something to show that the mother's work is important."

One afternoon Miss Addams chanced to walk along Polk Street as she returned from a sick-call. She crossed a busy street, then glanced east. On the steps of a shabby tenement an old woman sat in the April sunshine, quietly spinning. A shawl lay across gaunt shoulders; hands were thin and work-worn but they moved with assurance.

"That woman is not as old as she looks!" Jane thought tenderly. "She is aged by trouble." She paused by a doorway and watched deft fingers twirl the spindle as strong, smooth thread piled lightly in the woman's lap. Walking near, Jane decided to speak in a Sicilian dialect, she guessed that might be the right tongue.

"You make good thread," she said admiringly.

The woman's face lighted as though a candle had been set behind it. Her quick smile banished the look of age.

"This is the spindle my father made for me when I was a girl," she said. "*It* makes the good thread."

Instantly, as though God spoke to her, Jane Addams knew what she should do about the foreign mothers.

"Will you bring your spindle to Hull-House and show us how you spin?" she invited. "We'll have a party. You spin well. Many will like to watch you."

"Yes! I come!" the woman accepted quickly, speaking in the dialect Miss Addams had used. Then her face clouded. "But you will not want an old peasant woman, like me," she added.

"We want a good spinner—like you," Miss Addams answered. "I shall come by and let you know the day. Very soon."

Her new idea, announced at the supper table, grew rapidly. Many Hull-House ideas seem to spring quickly from tiny seeds, like Jack-and-the-beanstalk vines. The party was set for Friday evening and Ellen immediately began planning an exhibit of women's tools and lectures on the development of household labor.

"Not so fast!" Jane laughed. "This exhibit is for people —not for historical lectures."

"It's both," Ellen insisted. "You don't know what I found today. Within two blocks of our corner I've discovered four varieties of spindles and three sorts of spinning wheels. I was hunting them for my art class to draw."

"That reminds me," Jane said. "Remember that Irish spinning wheel you rescued, just as the owner's son was about to use it for kindling? I think I'm on the track of a Bohemian lad who knows wood carving and can repair it."

"Fine, and my class will help you," Ellen added. "We'll get the history of the tools worked out, too."

Jane was pleased—but not deflected from her major objective, to let the young people see their mothers honored. She stopped Angelina in the hall the next day and asked her to bring her mother on Friday evening.

"But why do you want my mother at Hull-House?" the Italian girl asked. Her brown eyes flashed; this was an odd invitation.

"Your mother can show us her skill in household . . ."

"My mother!" Angelina interrupted disdainfully. "My mother is an old peasant woman, she wears the babushka and her old-country dresses. She does her hair in a tight knot and she looks ugly. I love my mother," she added as an afterthought, "but she is better at home!"

"I see her differently, Angelina," Miss Addams replied

kindly. "Her babushka is a beautiful bit of cloth which she spun and wove herself. It is prettier than the silly hats my friends wear. I, too, wear my hair in a knot and like it that way. Your mother's native dress becomes her."

Angelina flushed, suspicious lest the lady was teasing her. Could it be possible that Miss Addams really wanted her mother—that old woman? But she saw this was not a joke.

"I'll bring her, Miss Addams," she decided. "But she is stupid. She cannot talk the English."

"We'll manage," Jane replied. "I speak Italian, you know. I'll like to visit with her."

On the evening of the party, Angelina was still dubious. She brought her mother, in babushka and shawl, but she left her at the back door. Angelina slipped around and entered at the front, alone. Miss Addams saw it all—she didn't miss much of what went on—but she said nothing to the girl for she understood her feeling.

Later in the evening Angelina's mother proved to be the star spinner, and the daughter, from the back of the room, saw the audience applaud as the mother, flushed, happy and looking years younger, twirled her spindle flashingly. When the party ended, Angelina and her mother left together, arm in arm.

Week by week the exhibit of textile tools grew, and there were more parties. Syrians, Russians, Italians, Irish and other groups illustrated various ways of spinning and weaving. The fame of those parties spread by word of mouth, often much exaggerated as the tale was told in one

language after another. Unexpected happenings resulted, as for instance the arrival of the Russian friends.

This group of Russian women worked in a sweatshop down Polk Street. After their long day's toil they dressed in their best and came to Hull-House to enjoy the party that they had heard was given every evening. Alas! That evening there was no party. Mary Keyser, always good in a pinch, dashed to the kitchen to prepare food. Jenny had stayed for supper and she helped with music and refreshments but the party dragged. Something disappointed their guests, and residents didn't know enough Russian to discover what was missing.

"Maybe you'd like to see our textile tools?" Ellen remarked finally and she led the way to the exhibit. The women seemed so weary, yet they did not leave.

The thirty tired women were transformed when they

entered that room. *This* was what they'd hoped to see. They rushed about exclaiming over a spinning frame and several sorts of spindles. They chattered happily, all fatigue gone. When they saw the spinning wheel they thought it a miracle of new invention. They had never seen such a tool in their part of Russia.

"Look! Look what I make! And no wheel either." One who spoke a little English caught Miss Addams's arm and then turned up her own skirt to show the handsome petticoat.

"This I make," she boasted. "Americans weave terrible stuff!"

"She means," Ellen said sadly, "that she works fourteen hours a day on that coarse cotton used for work clothes. A pity she has seen nothing beautiful that Americans produce."

From this beginning the idea of a Labor Exhibit grew. Later Hull-House became too crowded for all the activities, so Mr. Joseph T. Bowen built Bowen Hall, a large and handsome red brick building, fronting on Polk Street. This housed Boys' Clubs and provided an auditorium where Hull-House could hold meetings and concerts. But room was planned, too, for the exhibit of working tools by that time called 'The Labor Museum.' Ellen had her lectures on the growth of the textile industry and they proved popular.

All this led to the opening of a handicraft shop were Italian, Danish and Irish women made textiles—right there at Hull-House—and developed a self-supporting business. They did not stop with textiles, either. Soon they were making and selling pottery, metal work and wooden articles, crafts they had learned in their motherlands.

The labor exhibit turned out to be more than a bridge, it was a practical help to many families. As she heard the hum of activity in the shop, Jane Addams often thought of Canon Barnett at Toynbee Hall and the words he had spoken to her as she left London:

"The best way to help people is to help them to help themselves."

CHAPTER 11

❧ WHAT IS YOUR HOME? ❧

DURING THE EARLY DAYS of Hull-House, American cities were growing so fast that health needs were often neglected. Chicago was probably no better or worse than others, but certainly its garbage collection was careless. Jane Addams thought that the ugly, noisome, wooden garbage boxes fastened to the sidewalks were one of the hardest trials she had to endure. Open garbage boxes would be bad enough in any part of any city, but in the Nineteenth Ward in Chicago, that crowded area around Halsted and Polk Streets, they were dreadful.

Day after day, old garbage rotted and overflowed. Greek and Italian fruit peddlers tossed rotting left-overs on top of other trash. Immediately children gathered around, searching hopefully. If they were lucky they might find an apple or orange with one good bite remaining. (Jane Addams was often reminded of that scene in Mile End Road, in London, that had so affected her.) Rag-pickers who gathered trash at the city dump, sorted the stuff at home and then discarded the leavings onto the boxes. The horrid stink arising in summer was called "The smell of America" by those who did not know other parts of their new country.

On a good day, babies crawled on the sidewalks and clutched the sides of the boxes as they tried to stand erect. Children played around them. Boys searched the trash hopefully—occasionally a lucky lad found something he could use as a missile in the constant warfare with the older gangs.

Hull-House residents burned their own garbage in an incinerator they had devised. And as soon as adult clubs were organized, talks were given about cleanliness and city housekeeping.

"A city is different from your pretty village in the old country," Dr. Hamilton said over and over. "There, when you swept house-trash out-of-doors, sunshine and the geese took care of it. Here, in a city, it is different."

"But, Doctor," some woman was sure to speak up, "even though I attend to my own trash, there is still the garbage box." Yes, Dr. Hamilton had to admit, there was still the garbage box. One could smell it all through Hull-House.

So the residents decided to make a survey. They would see how garbage was handled in the entire Nineteenth Ward. Perhaps they could show a connection between lack of cleanliness and the high death rate. But surveys required workers and Hull-House people had no money for hiring them.

This idea for a survey came a while after the Hull-House Woman's Club was organized, and the residents decided to appeal to club members for help. So Jane Addams presented the idea at the next meeting.

"I burn my trash in my stove, Miss Addams," one member said defensively.

"I sweep my steps clean every morning," another retorted. "That is the end of my home."

"But is it, really?" Miss Addams asked her. The members looked at each other, surprised. Here was a new idea.

"Two rooms and the steps—that is my home," the club member repeated.

"That is your home, yes," Miss Addams agreed. "That is your own private place for your family. I am proud that you keep it clean. But does your home really end with your steps? Your children walk along the sidewalks, by the garbage boxes. Is not the walk a part of your home?"

The women were silent, thinking.

"Your husband goes to his work, far beyond this home and street and ward. Some of your friends live in other parts of the city—maybe the whole city is your home? When you take out your citizenship papers you learn about the state of Illinois and your chosen country, The United States of America. Isn't *that* your home?" These were wide thoughts.

In the silence a club member rose.

"I will help look after the garbage, Miss Addams," she volunteered.

"I could work three evenings a week," another promised.

Twelve helpers signed up that day and through the hot summer they inspected the collection of garbage. It was not easy to work all day washing, ironing, scrubbing and cooking and then inspect garbage boxes all evening. But the volunteers listed more than one thousand violations of existing laws. Chicago needed new laws of course, but it also needed enforcement of laws already on the books.

Backed by two business men, Jane Addams got the job of garbage inspector for her ward. She left Hull-House at six each morning to see that cart-drivers started out promptly. She followed wagons to make sure that they were not overloaded so that the contents dropped off on the way to the dump ground. She insisted on having more wagons and she got the dislike of city politicians who thought that a woman—with no vote—should not have a city job. Many foreign-born women agreed that a public job was no place for a woman. But she kept on with her work.

There was no magical change in either cleanliness or health—improvements seldom come rapidly. But there were a few gains. Now Americans saw that their neighbor-lady believed that when she took a political job she should do the work—a novel idea to many who thought of such a job as a "snap." The boxes no longer overflowed. Both the smell and the danger to health lessened.

In time, the wooden boxes were taken away and covered metal containers were used. The standard of cleanliness showed some improvement and gradually the health rating was better. The Hull-House Woman's Club was proud of its first venture into city housekeeping.

Unexpectedly, the effort to clean up the ward resulted in turning attention to its housing. Some of the volunteer inspectors had prospered and moved to other parts of the city. They were shocked when they came back and saw the tumbled down tenements and dirty alleys that once they had hardly noticed. One got a gang of boys to dig away the trash in her former alley. The boys dug off a foot of stuff and uncovered a good pavement, buried and long forgotten.

"This is like in Naples," an Italian boy laughingly boasted. "I never expected to find buried streets in Chicago!" The boys diligently cleaned up that block-long alley and immigrants who lived in shacks facing upon the revealed pavement were impressed. The volunteers determined to do something about the worst buildings.

The next time one of the residents was invited to a fashionable club to speak about Hull-House and its work she told the story of the buried alley and the tumbled-down houses and she mentioned the property-owner by name. Naturally he was annoyed when word got to him, and he came to reprove Miss Addams.

"What good would it do for me to fix up those houses —or put in plumbing?" he demanded. "Those people don't know how to take care of a bathroom!"

"I haven't a doubt but what you are right," she agreed with him quickly. (That was a disarming trait in Jane Addams. She could always see two sides of a question!) "But here at Hull-House, we have discovered that people can learn. You would be surprised!"

"I'll tell you what I'll do," he said quickly, annoyed that he had not convinced her, "I'll turn those buildings over to you. I'll give you a ten year lease. I now get two thousand dollars a year rent from that property. You may have it. But I warn you, it's a waste of money to spend it for improvements." He kept his promise and Hull-House residents studied their new problem. The owner was certainly right—only three or four of the buildings were worth improving.

"At least you will have the income for your work," a friend remarked to Jane Addams.

"Take money from such places!" Miss Addams was horrified. "I shall tear them down!"

"You can't do that!" the friend exclaimed. "If you deliberately throw away two thousand dollars a year, you can never again ask people for money for your work. Think again, Jane."

"I have thought," Jane replied quietly. "I shall tear the shacks down as soon as I can find places for the tenants to move into. If I never again can ask for gift money —well, I shall meet that trouble when it comes."

The three fairly good houses were sold and moved off the block. The rest were torn down. The ground was cleaned and rolled and made into the first playground in Chicago. The residents believed that it was the first large public playground in the country. And Jane Addams, her head held high, got more gifts of money for her work than before.

Now, at long last, the children in the Nineteenth Ward had a place to play. Hull-House groups used the playground for festivals of many sorts. Often it was gay with bright-colored costumes from many lands. Native songs drifted on the air and cheered many a shut-in who could not come to the festival.

The first of these many celebrations was a May Day party. A Maypole was set up and every Hull-House club was to have some part in the great occasion.

"Who's going to be Queen, Miss Jenny?" the small children asked.

"You have to have a Queen for May Day, Teacher."

"Of course we'll have a Queen," Jenny hastily agreed. "I'll tell you tomorrow how she is to be chosen."

That night there was a conference among the residents. As a result the Boys' Club spent an evening mysteriously cutting and bending stout wires which they stacked in the front hall. In the morning the contest for May Queen was announced.

"Each child is to have a wire," Miss Jenny told her children. "Older girls and boys are to have wires, too. Everyone can try to win. If a boy wins, he shall be King and wear a crown, too.

"These wires are your magic wands for trying-out. You hold them—so." She held a wire in her right hand. "The curved part is the handle, see? You push bits of paper onto your wire—look, I'll show you what I mean." She tossed some paper scraps onto the rug and speared them with the wire. "See? Shove paper onto the wire. The girl or boy who brings to us the most wires, packed full of paper trash picked up on the streets, wins the contest. That girl will be Queen. Or if a boy wins, we'll have a queen *and* a king for the party."

The children could hardly wait to get out onto the street and start work. Perhaps that contest was the strangest of all ways to elect a May Queen but the pretty little Italian girl who won the honor carried her scepter proudly, knowing that she had earned it by doing something for her neighborhood.

The whole ward, that May Day, looked neater than it had been in many a year. The crowds who flocked to the party admired the tidy gutters and walks. It is said that this contest was the first of all spring "Clean-up-Weeks" in Chicago and perhaps in any city. News of the contest and the selection of the queen was published across the country and eventually "Clean-up-Week" was celebrated nationally. Good city-housekeeping is very catching.

One of the delights at Hull-House was that workers never knew where a new idea would lead them. None had suspected that an attack on garbage would end with a playground and a national "Clean-up-Week." But still another result was even more heartening. People found that there was something to be done about their surroundings. A child could pick up papers. A grownup could see that laws were obeyed. Everyone could help make America beautiful.

CHAPTER 12

❧ HULL-HOUSE INFLUENCE ❧ GROWS

JANE ADDAMS FOUND that many people, near and far, wanted to hear about Hull-House and its neighbors. She often had to be away from the big house that she loved, but she was serving it in a new way when she made talks through the state, the nation, and finally in distance places around the world. She talked about health and housing; about children and their right to be educated and protected; about clean streets and food; about fair wages and safe working conditions—oh, she found much to talk about.

Eager listeners in both urban and rural communities gave a great deal of thought to her words. The social conscience of America had begun to stir feebly in the 1890's; after the turn of the century it was awakened. People saw that Jane Addams was no idle dreamer; she lived her ideals. Many thought that the kind neighborliness Hull-House practiced might be one of the ways to lessen poverty; might even bring about the American ideal of equality that had been written into the Declaration of Independence.

An even larger audience read what Miss Addams wrote for newspapers and magazines and for book publication. But at busy Hull-House it was hard to find quiet —life was exciting there. So she often went to Mrs. Bowen's well-ordered home for a couple of days of writing.

On a spring afternoon, she was returning from such a two-day stay when she got off the streetcar at the Polk Street corner. She had tucked her briefcase of papers under her arm and started toward Hull-House, when a young voice called to her.

"Oh, Miss Addams! Look!" She turned to smile at Theo Poulopolus, one of her Greek friends. "Look-it, Miss Addams! See what I've got?"

"Shoes, Theo!" She was properly surprised. "How shiny and beautiful they are."

"*New* and shiny!" he assured her proudly. "Look-it!" He put a hand on her brief case and gently edged her through the traffic to the sidewalk. There he bent down and ran a finger over the neat uppers. "Ain't they *nice*? I never had *new* American shoes before. My father is working steady now and he says he can get one of us kids a pair each pay-day. Nida gets hers next. Ain't they wonderful?" His face shone with pride and joy.

"I'm proud for you, Theo," she told him. "They are beautiful."

As she lingered, admiring, Jane Addams thought of

Theo's father—a fine, proud man. He would accept nothing but a chance to work and Hull-House had got him a job.

That evening she told the residents about the new shoes.

"Children love shoes, don't they?" she said as her tale ended. "I never thought until now how many songs and stories are about shoes—red shoes, fairy shoes, golden slippers and Cinderella's, made of glass."

"Shoes are so personal," some one at the table remarked.

"And so hard for the poor to get," Ellen Starr added.

"Just give Poulopolus a little time and he will have all his children shod," Florence Kelley said, briskly. "That man is a worker and his employer promised me he would have a steady job." She knew because she had got that work for Theo's father.

The immigrant naturally needed help in a strange land. But it took a midnight visitor to show Jane Addams that the city was bewildering even to a native-born American. One night she wakened, sensing a new sound. By the dim light from Halsted Street she saw the outline of a man, climbing in at her window.

"What do you want here?" she asked quietly. She was not frightened. A man at the window was nothing compared to that front door in Cedarville! It was the intruder who was startled.

"Money!" he said hoarsely. "You'd better be still, too!" he added as he whirled around to face her. She could not tell whether or not he had a gun, but she sat up straight and fearless—a quaint figure in a long-sleeved, high-neck nightgown.

"My purse is in the top drawer, on the right," she told him, "and do be quiet!"

He stared at her uneasily, then turned and opened the drawer.

"What are you doing this for?" Jane asked with frank curiosity. "You don't act like an experienced thief."

"I'm doing it because I am hungry—and I can't get a job," he cried, crossly.

"I could probably get you a job," the voice from the bed said kindly. "There, my purse is in that corner. You might dump out the money and leave the purse—it will be no good to you."

He obeyed her. But as he swept the money into his pocket a new idea came to him.

"You just want me to come back so you'll have the cops on me," he growled.

"That is a foolish way to talk, young man," she said. "You are not stealing anything that I would not give a hungry man. Take two dollars for a loan and leave the rest, if you like. You can return the money when you have your new job. Ask for Miss Addams when you come in the morning."

"Yes ma'am!" To his own astonishment, he selected two dollars and put the rest of the money on the dresser. Then he threw his leg over the window sill—ready to leave.

"Don't go out that way," Jane Addams whispered

sharply. "Someone might see you and think you were a thief. Go down the stairs—but carry your shoes. People are sleeping. No need to awaken anyone. I shall expect you at nine. Good night, my friend."

He stared at her, puzzled. But she was drawing up the covers, plainly the interview had ended.

"Yes, Ma'am," he said, meekly. He pulled off his ragged shoes, tucked them under his arm and softly closed the door behind him. She could barely hear his footsteps on the stairs and the gentle click of the front door closing.

"Perhaps he will not trust me," she thought as she settled to sleep. But he was there, promptly at nine the next morning. After two hours, she located a job for him. He paid back her loan. He was a skilled workman, who had not known how to find a job.

The Hull-House people came to see that better employment agencies were needed. So they worked through the few good agencies and routed out some of the dishonest ones. They began to work on a bill ordering state inspection of all employment agencies and they felt that the new law passed in 1899 would make a good start toward improvements.

In such ways, the work at Hull-House broadened. It was Robert Fulton, someone recalled, who long before had said: "When you find a need, seek how to meet it." Such a need was a Post Office sub-station—of all things! Immigrants were losing money, it was found, when they tried to send cash to kinfolk in the old country. Men who acted as agents either charged a high fee for getting a

postal money order downtown, or else they simply stole the whole sum entrusted to them. After Sub-station Number 10 opened at Hull-House the business was done near home.

Jane Addams worked for many causes that she hoped would help people: prohibition, woman's suffrage, better wages, improved relations between employers and employees, shorter hours of labor, safer factories, world peace. Some of these aims have been realized, some are still hopes for the future. Jane Addams was a leader in social thinking and so was often ahead of her times. But postponement of success did not discourage her. It made her search for new ways of making life better for all.

A few years after Jane Addams went to Hull-House, settlements were opened in New York, in Boston and other cities—and in other crowded neighborhoods in Chicago. These followed the pattern that Hull-House had tried and found good: an exchange of ideas and service between people of education and the poor, each wanting to learn.

On the day that a British scholar visited Chicago, people discovered that education was not always on one side. The visitor had asked to be taken to see Hull-House and in some way Jimmy O'Reilly heard of his coming and was standing on the steps of Hull-House when he arrived.

"Me grandmother can talk the way the newspaper says you can," he announced boldly.

The scholar paused and asked Jimmy a question in ancient Gaelic.

Jimmy grinned. "I can't talk it meself, but you sound like Granny," he said.

"Take me to her!" the visitor begged. They followed Jimmy down the block, into a back yard, up three flights of an outside stairway to Granny. Jimmy was right—she was the only person the visitor had found in America who could talk that old and almost forgotten tongue.

The luncheon at a downtown club had to wait while the visitor took down words and phrases that Granny spelled out for him. The whole neighborhood was proud. Miss Addams was pleased, but not surprised—something nice was always happening.

Jane Addams lived to be seventy-five years old and forty-five of those years were lived at Hull-House. She received many honors—the Nobel Peace Prize, several national awards and fifteen honorary degrees from colleges and universities. She often said that one occasion she greatly enjoyed was the day that the University of Wisconsin awarded her the degree of Doctor of Laws.

As the stirring words of the degree were read . . . "your eminence as a philanthropist, social reformer, author, creator of the world's greatest of all social settlements . . . recognized the world over . . ." she caught a glimpse of the gleaming dome of the Capitol. Memory flashed backward and she saw herself and George, there in Madison, on the happy day when they had stood under that dome, spellbound by Old Abe. The thrill of that journey came back and she felt close to the great man who had taught her to believe in a country where every man could be free to live and work and make his own happiness.

One of her memorable days was the celebration of the fortieth anniversary of the opening of Hull-House. Many former residents came from afar for a reunion.

Those who had been long away found great changes. Hull-House was now a group of a dozen buildings and covered most of a city block. The old Hull mansion, bereft of its porches, stood in the middle—a jewel in a sturdy setting. The new entrance hallway led into the high-ceilinged rooms where Jane and Ellen and Mary had first begun their housekeeping.

Visitors saw that people of many races and walks of life came and went as before. Once most of those who came were immigrants who spoke in a strange tongue. Now most were Americans who spoke with hardly a trace of accent. But the spirit of the place was unchanged.

Glowing reports were heard of the joy that the Joseph T. Bowen Country Club was bringing to Hull-House neighbors. This club was given by Mrs. Bowen in 1912 as a memorial to her husband. For weeks, Miss Addams and Mrs. Bowen had searched for the perfect spot for a camp. Finally they decided upon seventy-two acres of wooded hills and ravines north of Chicago, near Waukegan, Illinois. Mrs. Bowen had built houses for living and had provided all sorts and kinds of recreational facilities. The place was so large that whole clubs could vacation at the same time. Acquaintance begun at Hull-House grew into life-long friendship as girls and boys played together in beautiful out-of-door surroundings.

Residents who had come had admired the changes and talked for hours about their successes and failures in the fascinating search for new and better ways of helping people to find a good life. The celebration seemed like an Old Home Week in a small town. Indeed, that neighborhood really was a kind of small town set in a great city.

By this year, 1930, people were beginning to see that a city, with all its disadvantages, had much to give, provided a man could make friends and learn city ways. Many former neighbors, once poor and forlorn, were now successful and had made homes in other parts of the city. Proud and happy, they came back to Hull-House for the reunion. In their new locations they were no longer called "immigrants" nor were they "Poles" or "Greeks" or "Bohemians"—they had become Americans and their lives were woven into the fabric of national life as bright threads are woven into a tapestry. Their children hardly remembered the first hard years. Their children's children might never know the difficulties of coming to a new land.

But though many had moved away, the Nineteenth Ward was ever crowded with newcomers, needing friends and neighbors. Mexicans came after the revolution of 1911. Negroes moved up from the south. A drifting population from over the nation made this section their starting place in a great city. Life at Hull-House was an unending search for a better life for Theo and Rebecca, Toni and Eve, for Alex and Juan.

After many of the Hull-House family had told their stories of work done, modest Jane Addams rose to talk to her friends. She praised the new ideals and the new causes. But were the ideas really so new, she wondered?

"Social ideals are as old as the Bible," she reminded them. "As old as the commandment, 'Love thy neighbor as thyself.' "

Then, the reunion over, everyday work was resumed—and continues to the present time.

As the crowds drifted away from that celebration the name of Jane Addams was heard more often than any of the others—famous though many were.

"There is a woman who knew what she wanted to do and persisted toward an ideal that she never lost," one said as he stepped into a handsome automobile and drove away.

"Miss Addams, she is a fine lady," the policeman remarked at the corner, as he held up traffic so that the car could move north.

"Never was one like her," a Polish grandmother told her children when they brought news of the departing guests.

"She is my neighbor and friend," a young Greek mother said. That would have pleased Jane Addams more than all the speeches.

✌ EPILOGUE ✌

Among Jane Addams' books are:

TWENTY YEARS AT HULL-HOUSE

THE SECOND TWENTY YEARS AT HULL-HOUSE

THE SPIRIT OF YOUTH AND THE CITY STREETS

THE LONG LANE OF WOMAN'S MEMORY

PEACE AND BREAD IN TIME OF WAR

DEMOCRACY AND SOCIAL ETHICS

THE EXCELLENT BECOMES PERMANENT

A NEW CONSCIENCE AND AN ANCIENT EVIL

A few of the internationally known people who have been residents at Hull-House are:

Mackenzie King, Prime Minister of Canada

Francis W. Parker, Educator

Robert A. Woods, Head of East End House, Boston

Charles Zeublin, Pioneer in Adult Education

Frances Perkins, U. S. Secretary of Labor

Lillian Wald, Founder of Henry Street Settlement,
New York

Mary E. MacDowell, University of Chicago Settlement

Judge Julian W. Mack, Judge of the Juvenile Court

Prince Kropotkin, Writer on the Russian Peasants

T. G. Masaryk, President of Czechoslovakia

Some of the Honors and Awards Given to Jane Addams

Awarded fifteen honorary degrees by Colleges and Universities.

1909, President of the National Conference of Charities and Correction (First woman to hold this office).

1915, President of the Woman's Peace Party.

1919, The name of this organization was changed to Woman's International League for Peace and Freedom. Jane Addams was president until her death.

1928, President of the Pan-Pacific Woman's Union.

1930, Awarded the *Medal of Military Merit* by the Greek Republic for her services to the fatherland during the period of the World War (1914–1918).

1931, First on a list of twelve leading women of America and awarded top prize by *Good Housekeeping Magazine.*

1931, Picked as one of the six leading Americans.

(These two 'lists' started a series of many other lists of leading Americans on which Jane Addams' name was always included.)

1931, Awarded the Thomas M. Carey Prize of $5,000 by Bryn Mawr College for Eminent Achievement.

1931, From Bryn Mawr, Jane Addams went to Rockford College where she spoke at the fiftieth anniversary of her graduation. In her address that day she said: "May I warn you against doing good to people and trying to make others good by law? One does good, if at all, *with* people, not *to* people. . . . Democracy is . . . a process according to which we do not force law upon others but make it for ourselves."

1931, October, Awarded $5,000 by *Pictorial Review Magazine* as 'the most outstanding woman of the year.' (She gave $500 of this amount to the Chicago Community Relief Fund and the rest to Hull-House for current expenses which were very heavy during the depression.)

1940, Honored by the United States Government as one of thirty-five chosen for the Famous American Commemorative Issue. Hers was a ten cent stamp with her picture.

Born, October 6, 1860. Died, May 21, 1935.

College of St. Mary of the Springs Library